Agile Working and Well-Being in the Digital Age

Christine Grant · Emma Russell
Editors

Agile Working and Well-Being in the Digital Age

palgrave
macmillan

Editors
Christine Grant
School of Psychological, Social and
Behavioural Sciences
Coventry University
Coventry, UK

Emma Russell
University of Sussex Business School
(USBS)
University of Sussex
Brighton, UK

ISBN 978-3-030-60282-6   ISBN 978-3-030-60283-3   (eBook)
https://doi.org/10.1007/978-3-030-60283-3

Cover illustration: © Melisa Hasan

This Palgrave Macmillan imprint is published by the registered company Springer Nature
Switzerland AG
The registered company address is: Gewerbestrasse 11, 6330 Cham, Switzerland

To Bill, Gabriella and my mum and dad for their constant support and motivation

—Christine Grant

To my lovely family, thanks for your enduring support

—Emma Russell

Foreword

From the 1980s and 1990s, technology-enabled working, at distance from main organisational locations, has grown in sophistication, numbers of workers participating in such working practices and range of occupations covered. In 2020 in particular, we have seen a massive and rapid shift to home and other forms of tech-enabled working because of the pandemic of 2019/2020. At the time of writing, extensive tech-enabled working from remote locations may become the 'new normal' for some, and a temporary form of business continuity for others, as flare-ups cause local lockdowns.

Against this backdrop, this edited collection provides a timely and up-to-date overview of key issues on the human experience of agile working, a form of working that encompasses temporal and spatial flexibility and the use of technologies, to address organisational and worker needs. Understanding the human experience is fundamental to effective tech-enabled working: time and again, research has revealed that ignoring the human side of technology leads to sub-optimal solutions that force the soft machine (human) to adapt to the hard machine (technology). Accordingly, agile working can pose many challenges, including threats to well-being from work intensification, blurring of work/home boundaries, email (and other forms of technology) addiction, an always on culture, digital surveillance and social isolation.

Providing a range of relevant resources in one collection, the book's chapters cover key topics pertinent to managing the challenges of agile working, such as home/work boundary management, distractions from new communications technologies, promoting physical activity in remote and sedentary workers, competencies required by digital workers, team-working, leadership and the use of space.

Engaging and intelligently written, the collection covers current research, future research needs and guidance on implementing agile working. As such, the book will be of interest to researchers, practitioners in human resource management and management consulting, postgraduate and advanced undergraduate students studying the nature of contemporary working practices.

August 2020

Kevin Daniels
Professor of Organizational Behaviour
Norwich Business School
University of East Anglia
Norwich, Norfolk, UK

ACKNOWLEDGEMENTS

This book started as a seed of an idea two years ago, an aspiration to explore the effects of digitisation on our lives. I would like to thank Emma for making this a reality, providing a supporting voice through every step; working together has been effortless, innovative and kept me sane through a global pandemic, this book is better for our every conversation. I would also like to thank every chapter author for their contribution; fresh minds and new insights equal fascinating reading. Finally, thank you to my husband Bill and daughter Gabriella, for giving me space to work extra hours, my eternal sounding boards, being the best support team I could wish for, and for never doubting this could be real.

Agile working can only be a success with an open mind, tools to make it work and an ability to embrace change; I hope those reading this book will find a fresh approach.

—Dr. Christine Grant (August 2020)

This has been such an interesting and enjoyable project, and there are several people I would especially like to thank. Firstly, to our chapter authors who produced such insightful and original work, were open to suggestions and amazingly met all of our deadlines. Thank you—it has been a pleasure to work with you. Secondly, to the organisations and colleagues I work with, who have really informed my understanding of best practice in agile work, and how this can be effectively applied in the context of real-world constraints and demands.

Next, to Chris. What can I say? For your support, supreme organisational skills, intellect and drive—thank you. I have loved working on this with you. I look forward to our next collaboration.

Finally, to J, Isobel and Harry—thank you for your endless support and pride in what I do, and for being the best part of every day.

—Dr. Emma Russell (August 2020)

CONTENTS

Part VI   Conclusions

Notes on Contributors

Dr. Kelly A. Basile is an Assistant Professor of Management at Emmanuel College in Boston, MA. Her research interests include work-life boundary management, technology, culture and diversity in organizations. In addition to her academic experience, Kelly worked in commercial research and consulting for over a decade.

Professor T. Alexandra Beauregard is a Chartered Psychologist and Professor of Organizational Psychology at Birkbeck College, University of London. Her research focuses on the work-life interface, flexible working arrangements and diversity management. Alexandra is an editor for the journal Work, Employment and Society and an Executive Board member of the Work and Family Researchers Network.

Dr. Petros Chamakiotis is an Associate Professor of Management at ESCP Business School in Madrid, Spain, and the Chair of the IFIP WG 9.5 'Our Digital Lives'. He explores connectivity and virtual working, the role of technology in emergencies, and online (health) communities. His work has been published in outlets such as *Information Systems Journal* and *International Journal of Information Management*.

Dr. Maria Charalampous is a Lecturer in Business and Occupational Psychology at Coventry University. She has a long-standing interest in remote e-working and how working at anyplace and anytime can influence individuals' well-being. Maria is a qualified psychometrician and has developed a multidimensional scale that allows organisations, managers and individuals to examine remote e-workers' well-being.

Carl Clarke, Chartered FCIPD, is an experienced Human Resources Director with a demonstrated history of working in the energy, power and telecommunications sectors, in the UK and internationally. He has a passion for inclusion, culture, change, resilience, well-being, technology and supporting people and organisations succeed. Carl holds an MSc in Occupational Psychology from Coventry University and is a Chartered Member of the Institute of Personnel and Development.

Dr. Michelle Cleveland is a Senior Lecturer in Psychology at the University of Winchester where she is a member of the Social and Organisational Research Group. Her research has primarily focused on experiences of emotion and the coping strategies utilised by employees in various work-related contexts.

Deepali D'mello is an Organisational Psychologist and a PhD student at the University of Sussex. Her research interest is in understanding people's personality at work, their behaviour, and motivations to manage their work-related digital communications in relation to their productivity and personal well-being.

Dr. Christine Grant is a Chartered and Registered Occupational Psychologist and Deputy Head of School at Coventry University. She is a leading applied researcher in the psychology of remote e-working and agile working. Her work explores the impact of technology on remote e-workers work-life balance, job effectiveness and well-being, with an interest in developing new measures and related interventions for employees and employers, including the recently published E-Work Life scale. Christine has secured research funding with the ESPRC, British Psychological Society and many others. She has also worked across sectors with a wide range of organisations as an external consultant. Recently, she contributed to British Psychological Society's Covid19 crisis working group 'working differently' and the government's expert consultation on the coronavirus pandemic. Her work is disseminated widely through journals, conferences, practitioner guidance and in the media.

Dr. Rhiannon Jones is a Senior Lecturer in Psychology at the University of Winchester where she specialises in Cognitive Neuroscience and co-leads the Brain and Cognition Research

Group. Her primary research interest is the biological basis of cognitive biases in psychopathology.

Alessandra Mossa   is a chartered architect and a PhD student in Management at the University of Sussex. Her research interests include the social and spatial impacts of digital technologies on cities, regional and local impact of tourism, planning history and culture, community planning, filmic and graphic representation.

Dr. Rachel Nayani is a Lecturer in Organisational Behaviour and Human Resource Management at the University of East Anglia who has expertise on work, behaviour and sustainable well-being. Rachel undertakes research for the UK national What Works Centre for Well-being at Work. Her research primarily involves understanding organisational practices or combinations of practices for sustainable well-being and enhanced productivity at work.

Dr. Emma Russell is a Chartered and Registered Occupational Psychologist and a Senior Lecturer at the University of Sussex Business School (USBS). Emma is a member of the ESRC Digital Futures at Work Research Centre and Course Director for the MSc in Occupational and Organizational Psychology. Emma's research focuses on work-email activity, and its relationship with personality, well-being, resources and goal achievement. Emma has been funded by the ESRC, Acas, the NHS, RBT and others. She disseminates her research in high impact journals, conference papers, practitioner publications and the wider media. Emma is a member of the editorial board for the Journal in Organizational Behavior.

Anthony Thompson is a Lecturer in Business and Occupational Psychology at Coventry University, whose research area is workplace physical activity and sedentary behaviour. Prior to becoming a lecturer, Anthony worked as an independent business psychology consultant supporting organisations to achieve their strategic goals.

Professor Maria Uther is a Professor of Psychology at the University of Wolverhampton where she heads the Centre for Psychological Research. Her research is in the field of auditory perception and digital technologies and she is a HCPC registered occupational psychologist.

LIST OF TABLES

PART I

What is Agile Working?

CHAPTER 1

Introduction to Agile Working and Well-Being in the Digital Age

Emma Russell and Christine Grant

Abstract We are living in a digital age where work is now organised around the widespread use of information and communication technologies (ICT). In response to this, the concept of agile working has emerged, which involves liberating individuals from traditional forms of work and is arranged around four key activities. These involve promoting temporal and spatial flexibility, integrating resources, engaging in innovative activity and utilising communication and digital technology, in order to respond dynamically to service and market needs and to meet both individual and organisational goals. In this chapter, we discuss the four activities in agile working and comment on how these effect the performance and

E. Russell (✉)
University of Sussex Business School (USBS), University of Sussex,
Brighton, UK
e-mail: emma.russell@sussex.ac.uk

C. Grant
School of Psychological, Social and Behavioural Sciences,
Coventry University, Coventry, UK
e-mail: christine.grant@coventry.ac.uk

3

well-being of people at work. We then outline how each of the chapters in 'Agile Working and Well-being in the Digital Age' contribute understanding to this new work phenomenon, to inform students, researchers and practitioners about current and emerging trends in agile working, and how these now need to be tackled.

Keywords Digital age · Digitalisation · Agile working · Smart working · Boundary management · Innovation · Technology · Resources

1.1   Agile Working
and Well-Being in the Digital Age

We are currently living in a digital age. This unique period in history utilises digital technology to enable the mass production and dissemination of information through high-speed, widely accessible devices, software and infrastructure. The digital age largely emerged with the widespread use of the World Wide Web and increased broadband and Wi-Fi access; today many social, economic and organisational activities depend on information and communication technologies (ICT) to provide access to work and support working life. In April 2020, it was reported that 4.6 billion people across the globe are now active users of the Internet, with 3.5 billion people owning a smartphone [4]. Against this backdrop, we have begun to observe a burgeoning appetite amongst workers and organisations to capitalise on the digital revolution and promote new ways of working.

Agile working (sometimes referred to as 'smart' working) reflects this new movement. Originally a term developed by the software industry to refer to the need to develop more flexible and business-responsive technological infrastructure, it has since been adopted by practitioners and organisations who are interested in the human side of work. In recent years, think tanks (e.g. the Agile Alliance, the Agile Future Forum, the Work Foundation), professional organisations (e.g. the Chartered Institute for Personnel and Development: CIPD) and business journals (e.g. *Harvard Business Review: HBR, HR Magazine, the Wall Street Journal*) have devoted attention to the concept of agile working and how this can be used to benefit both organisations and workers. In particular, a focus of early implementer organisations has been on reducing costs whilst increasing productivity and supporting greater flexibility for workers. These institutions have considered using agile working practices to respond to and anticipate the needs of workers, organisations, markets and customers in a way that enables effective goal achievement, performance and productivity. However, the well-being of the workers who adopt agile working practices has largely been overlooked as a key focal area. This is likely due to the concept of agile working receiving minimal attention from academic researchers interested in the 'human' side of work, e.g. in psychology, organisational studies and HRM research. Traditionally, such scholars would consider well-being as a key outcome for understanding work practices. Because the academic literature relating to agile working in these fields has lagged well behind research in other domains, so too has the focus on well-being.

Despite a lack of attention paid to agile working in 'human' studies research, scholars in these fields *have* focused on a number of emerging working practices that are agile in nature, such as remote e-working [9]. Accordingly, where there is a 'human' focus, research has identified how well-being is affected by new modes of work, even if these have not previously been conceptualised under the banner of 'agile working'. This is a vital consideration when we consider that well-being at work has such a significant impact on the healthy functioning of individuals and organisations, with a direct impact on the bottom line [7, 17]. In this book, we refer to well-being as a multi-faceted construct involving the experience of pleasurable emotions and broader meaningful functioning (e.g. in relation to satisfaction, growth, accomplishment and engagement) [20, 28].

In 'Agile Working and Well-being in the Digital Age', we therefore take a human focus to understanding agile working and specifically address how it impacts well-being in this era of increased digital and communication technology. Our main aims are:

- To define agile working and introduce readers to its interrelated activities.
- To consider how well-being (as per the definition above) *along-side* productivity, performance and goal attainment outcomes has informed understanding of agile working practices, and how these can be optimised.
- To bring together the 'human' research and theories that have been used to make sense of agile working practices to date, whilst examining future pathways for research.

- To consider some of the significant issues, particularly in relation to well-being, that have arisen as worthy of research attention, in relation to agile working.

Each of the chapters in this book addresses these aims in different ways, which we outline towards the end of the Introduction. Our intention within this book is to introduce readers to the human side of agile working, and to elucidate how agile working practices impact well-being as a potentially 'forgotten' construct in the initial conceptualisations of agile work. Whilst providing a scholarly overview of the research field and recommending future directions, our authors also highlight how agile working practices can be optimally implemented, for practitioners and professionals involved in the design of agile working today.

1.2   What Is Agile Working?

We take a human view of agile working to provide a novel definition that encompasses, for the first time, four key interrelated activities of agile work. Following a review of both academic and 'grey' literature [11, 18, 24, 25], we state that:

Agile working involves liberation from traditional ways of organising and structuring work by:

  i. *Promoting temporal and spatial flexibility,*
 ii. *Integrating resources (people, knowledge, skills, facilities, infrastructure),*
iii. *Engaging in innovative activities,*
 iv. *Utilising new communication and digital technologies,*

to respond dynamically to evolving work, service and market priorities and to produce outputs that espouse core work and personal values towards achieving core work and organisational goals.

This definition provides a backdrop for exploring the issues related to agile working, in particular issues related to well-being. To be fully agile, and accrue the benefits of this type of working, an organisation would need to ensure that all of the four activities are undertaken, with success judged in terms of whether personal, work and organisational goals are met, whilst pursuing a future-focused customer/market-led agenda. The four agile working activities are now outlined below.

1.2.1   Promoting Temporal and Spatial Flexibility

Inherent within our definition is the notion that agile working challenges traditional structures and boundaries and traditional ways in which work performance is appraised. This means that in truly agile workplaces, individuals are encouraged to work at times and places that best suit them, the needs of the customer and the global marketplace. It is unlikely that agile workers would work in the same way, e.g. within 'normal office hours' from 9 a.m. to 5 p.m. Agile organisations give workers the flexibility to work differently, e.g. applying agreed contracted hours in a more flexible manner and from a suitable location base. For example, to fit in with caring requirements, a worker may start work at 10am. If a worker needs to contact a customer in a different time zone, then they may be working on a device in the evening, e.g. a tablet, smartphone, laptop, etc. If a worker lives a long way from their central shared office space, it may be more efficient for them to work from home, or in a local co-working hub. Such practices reflect the changing needs of an increasingly diverse workforce and marketplace and are all viable options for agile working. The transition from traditional to flexible temporal and spatial boundaries has given rise to a wide range of flexible working practices that have been extensively referenced and studied within the human studies research literature [14]. Telecommuting, remote working, homeworking, distributed working, e-working and flexitime are all concepts that have dealt with the notion that traditional working times and locations are moveable in modern agile work. Being able to work anytime, anyplace, anywhere is a central ethos to proponents of agile working.

1.2.2   Integrating Resources

The second key activity considers how resources can be utilised and optimised in agile working. A key output in agile working involves dynamically responding to and anticipating the needs of the customer and the markets, which means that traditional structures for integrating resources (e.g. within static departments and teams, or centralised office spaces) can become obsolete. By focusing on goals rather than functions, teams may now be brought together from across the globe, according to the specific skills, knowledge and talents of the constituent members, in relation to current projects [12]. Once a project goal is attained, the team may be disbanded [1]. Equally, if workers are operating outside of the traditional office, they may find that their home set-up does not necessarily offer the same access to equipment, social contact, technical support, etc. As such, resources may be more appropriately accessed by working from local hubs. Further, organisations may need to consider the extent to which it is their responsibility to provide home-based workers with appropriate, safe resources and equipment.

1.2.3   Engaging in Innovative Activities

The third key activity refers to the need to be innovative and creative in the way that we work. In order to be future-focused and pre-emptive and to take advantage of the blurring of boundaries, pioneering work patterns, contracts and activities have been developed. To a certain extent, the much maligned 'gig economy' has been borne from the need to be innovative in restructuring work contracts, taking on workers as and when they are needed and resulting in high levels of work precarity [13]. However, other innovative patterns, such as the four-day week (on full pay) or the '5-in-7' work pattern, have emerged and been lauded by organisations and workers alike. Forming, disbanding and then reforming teams, comprising different workers from different cultures, can also afford opportunities for enhancing creativity [27]. When team members are diverse in knowledge, skills, perspective, values, etc., this can encourage a hotbed of imagination, inspiring more ingenious solutions, compared to those working in comfortably static arrangements with the same familiar faces [27].

Of all of the activities involved in agile work, the extent to which agile working practices encourage a more innovative approach has arguably been the least well researched. Comparing outputs from virtual project teams with static physical teams could be one way of exploring the extent to which innovation evolves from agile working, and the extent to which any such innovation ultimately impacts worker well-being and organisational effectiveness. In 2014, the CIPD [3] suggested that whilst many organisations were keen to embrace agile working, their focus was predominantly on cutting costs and adhering to governance and compliance issues. Becoming agile, in order to become more innovative, was a consideration often excluded. Yet, agile working advocates espouse that work today should be less about short-term quantity of product or service, and more about the achievement of long-term key organisational goals and worker well-being. This means that the relentless execution of tasks is considered old hat, compared to giving people the time and space to be more creative, open-minded and foresighted. Ironically, such practices are likely to have a significant positive impact on the bottom line. In 2019, for example, Microsoft Japan announced that their month-long innovative experiment, which gave employees full pay for working a 4-day week, resulted in substantial productivity benefits. Compared to the same month of the previous year, sales rose by 40%, electricity consumption reduced by 23% and printed page production reduced by 59%. Workers were encouraged to use their day off to rest, engage in volunteering work or pursue a hobby. Researchers suggest that it is having the 'time and space' to switch off from work and engage different parts of the brain that help to promote this increased productivity and well-being [6]. This indicates how the creative and innovative repercussions of agile working warrant more research attention.

1.2.4   Utilising New Communication and Digital Technologies

The fourth major activity that defines agile working is the utilisation of digital technology to enable and support all other aspects of working practice. As technology evolves, so too do agile working practices. The advent of work extendable technologies (WETs) has been a particular game-changer as portable devices, such as tablets, laptops and smart-phones, have enabled people to access (and be accessed by) work well beyond traditional boundaries. As long as there is Wi-Fi or 4G/5G access, workers can connect to colleagues and work systems today in a way never before encountered. File sharing is enabled by rapid extensions of cloud-based services, and all forms of communication, from text-based to face-to-face meetings, are facilitated by both early tech (email/text) and state-of-the-art applications, such as enterprise social media (Zoom, Skype, Google Meet/Hangouts, MS Teams, Slack, Jabber, Yammer, etc.). It is compelling that the Office for National Statistics (ONS) announced that 30% of working people in the UK had worked from home during 2019, but that rates of home working differed significantly between sectors. The 'information and communication' and 'scientific activity and professional' sectors were more likely to work from home and be provided with the WET devices to do so. Clearly, being involved in digital, 'knowledge' work, and having organisational support and provision to facilitate home working, meant that these workers found it much easier to transition between home and office-based work. Yet, by 2018, although many workers had been given the opportunity to work from home, there were still sectors and organisations that had not taken advantage of the digital explosion to promote agile practices (only a 2% increase in homeworking from 2008 to 2018, according to ONS).

In 2020, the world was faced with the global coronavirus pandemic, which, for the first time, forced many workers and organisations to 'go agile', as lockdown measures were imposed by national governments. Suddenly, if organisations wanted their workers to keep working, they needed to invest in digital technology to enable this. In April 2020, the ONS reported that, as a result of workplace social distancing measures, 49% of adults in employment were working from home. In 2020, Ofcom announced that Zoom, which had 659,000 users registered pre-lockdown, had achieved 13 million users by April 2020 as people attempted to reclaim face-to-face contact in their new lockdown state. It is widely predicted that in a post-COVID world, investment in digital infrastructure will continue to surge, to allow more flexible working that transcends temporal and spatial boundaries. Leading the way are Twitter and Google, who both announced in 2020 that they will be happy for people to predominantly work from home, whenever their jobs allow, indefinitely.

1.3   What Issues Arise from Agile Working?

There is little doubt then that the move towards agile working shows little sign of abating. Yet, many organisations are currently only 'dabbling' by introducing some easy to implement agile practices (e.g. homeworking or offering flexible working hours) but not others (e.g. supporting innovation by providing 'creative' time). This is reflected in the use of agile working terminologies that specifically refer to aspects of remote work (see Chapter 2 for more). A HBR report in 2018 suggests that when organisations go 'fully agile' their productivity can increase by 60%, a compelling rationale for continuing this trend. But there is also research evidence to show that agile working is not necessarily a panacea that can cure all of our working ills. In relation to each of the four key agile working activities, we can see a range of issues emerging from the research literature that suggest negative impacts on well-being.

Agile working can provide organisations and workers with clear benefits, including increased productivity and a flexible approach to working hours that can positively impact workers' experience. However, there are several issues that need attention. Firstly, as agile working blurs temporal and spatial boundaries, research has examined the extent to which work-home balance is maintained. With the ability to be constantly connected, an 'always on' culture has emerged, promoting longer hours and an intensification of work activity [14, 21]. Whilst this might offer short-term benefits to employers, the negative impact on well-being is clear. Being unable to psychologically detach from work or engage in recovery and respite activities is seen to be one of the major tribulations of our times, creating sleep dysfunction, stress and longer-term absenteeism and ill health [22]. Further, presenteeism (working when unwell) can also affect productivity and is hard to manage from a distance when employees become less visible [15].

When working remotely, a number of issues arise relating to the visibility, health and support provided to workers. For example, workers can become isolated, lonely and demotivated [5, 8]. Being out of the office can also result in missed developmental and networking opportunities, and lower levels of visibility that can be synonymous with absence [15]. There are also concerns here with regard to physical health, with remote workers being more susceptible to sedentary behaviours and poor dietary habits [26].

Remote working can also inhibit knowledge sharing and creativity, which research suggests is a result of workers becoming isolated in their homes without the stimuli to support divergent thinking [23]. It is within social hubs that creativity and innovation are most likely to flourish. Virtual and global project teams can facilitate this, as cultural, social, knowledge and skills diversity can spring from agile working in this way. However, virtual teams need to be managed in non-traditional ways, potentially using a hybrid of leadership approaches to avoid the tendency for miscommunication and interpretation, and problems in co-ordinating activity [10].

Finally, and in relation to the explosion of digital technology, the research literature has demonstrated how digital interruptions, information overload and altered norms for virtual communication have depleted workers' resources and negatively impacted their well-being. The exponential increase in digital communication now means that workers are exposed to a continuous stream of interruptions throughout their working day if they keep their alerts switched on, which can negatively impact working memory and a sense of being in control of one's work [19]. Further, with information being disseminated so easily through digital channels, workers are reporting significant levels of stress and overload [2]. Recent research has also begun to focus on the new norms of negotiating new communication methods that is creating more emotional labour through more conscious self-regulation of our activities. When resources are low and self-regulation is depleted, people may be more likely to engage in problematic behaviours, such as incivility [16].

1.4   THE STRUCTURE OF THIS BOOK

In providing the first comprehensive overview of the research literature relating to how well-being is impacted by agile working practices, we hope that this book will offer a 'one-stop-shop' for readers wanting to understand: (i) the current state of play in relation to 'human' focused agile working research, (ii) where research needs to focus next and (iii) how agile working practices can best be implemented in future. By applying a human focus, our attention is not given to the more structural, governance, technological and economic issues associated with agile working. Rather, we examine the human experience of agile working, in terms of how it helps people to work effectively and optimise well-being. We attempt to cover all activities involved in agile working in this book, whilst acknowledging that more research is available in relation to remote working and the impact of digital technology on well-being, with less research currently available in regard to how agile working has resulted in more innovation and creativity.

We structure the book into sections as follows.

1.4.1   What Is Agile Working?

Following this introductory chapter, Grant uses Chapter 2 to discuss the different terms, concepts and practices associated with agile working and considers options for 'measuring' these phenomena in order to better understand workers' agile working experiences.

1.4.2   Managing Boundaries

In Chapter 3, Basile and Beauregard discuss the main theoretical underpinnings of boundary management, highlighting which temporal, spatial and structural boundaries are especially pertinent in agile work.

1.4.3   Managing Digital Communications

Central to facilitating agile working is the use of digital and communication technologies. In Chapter 4, Russell discusses the paradox of work-email and how individual differences in traits and goal pursuit can explain some of the contradictory findings in relation to well-being. In Chapter 5, Uther, Cleveland and Jones report on the physiological responses we demonstrate in response to digital notifications, and how the mode and the meaning of our alerts can create different stress responses. D'mello draws on some of the principles from the Managing Boundaries section to then discuss in Chapter 6 how workers are starting to regain control over their digital communications by applying forms of 'E-Resistance' as a means of bolstering their resources.

1.4.4   Healthy, Effective and Sustainable Agile Working

Charalampous discusses five facets of well-being in Chapter 7 that are impacted by agile working. In this chapter, she explains the importance of differentiating between different well-being factors, and what we can learn from the research undertaken in these five areas to date. Thompson then moves on in Chapter 8 to discuss the modern scourge of sedentary working, which blights many desk-bound workers but especially those who work remotely. Discussing the latest research into how health behaviours can be better promoted, this chapter offers important guidance for workers and managers alike. In Chapter 9, Clarke and Grant outline an e-competency framework that has been developed for agile organisations. Providing managers with some concrete guidance on the skills, knowledge, attributes and behaviours required for workers to be able to agile work effectively, this framework offers a sustainable way of encouraging healthy agile working.

1.4.5   Dynamic and Innovative Approaches to Effectively Managing and Sharing Resources

In a fascinating overview of the research into virtual teams, in Chapter 10, Chamakiotis discusses the nature of online teamwork, highlighting potential pitfalls and how such teams can best be managed to optimise creative and effective output. Relatedly, in Chapter 11, Nayani looks at how leadership models for managing distributed workers (including oft-ignored so-called blue-collar groups) require a novel, blended approach, to ensure the health and well-being of employees. Finally, in Chapter 12, Mossa considers how co-working hubs and collectives appear to offer a number of solutions for sharing resources and building a sense of belonging and identity for agile workers. Her insights indicate that to allow for an authentic agile experience, such hubs are likely to flourish when they are divorced from large corporate entities seeking only to commercialise the trend.

1.4.6   Conclusions

In the final chapter, Grant and Russell provide concluding comments, outlining key contributions of the book, principles for implementing agile working practices and indicating future pathways for developing agile working research and practice.

1.5   SUMMARY

Agile working is a popular premise that has received a great deal of positive press in recent years, with think tank surveys suggesting that more and more organisations want to embrace agile working with the many gains it appears to offer in terms of job performance, productivity, greater job satisfaction and benefits to well-being. Yet, operationalising agile working is not always easy, and academic research into the field tends to focus on specific agile working practices, rather than agile working as a whole. If organisations want to truly embrace agile working, they need to move away from purely bottom-line concerns and consider the opportunities that can be had by encouraging workers to flourish, be responsive, to find time to be creative. Promoting activities that engender well-being and sustainability will not only result in a healthier workforce, but longer term is also likely to produce significant organisational and personal benefits. With this book, our aim is to equip researchers and practitioners with the information and insights to help develop effective agile working practices now, and to understand what more needs to be done to develop agile working and well-being in the next tranche of the digital age.

REFERENCES

1. Ammeter, A. P., & Dukerich, J. M. (2002). Leadership, team building, and team member characteristics in high performance project teams. *Engineering Management Journal, 14*(4), 3–10. https://doi.org/10.1080/10429247. 2002.11415178.
2. Barley, S. R., Meyerson, D. E., & Grodal, S. (2011). Email as a source and symbol of stress. *Organization Science, 22*(4), 887–906. https://doi.org/ 10.1287/orsc.1100.0573.
3. CIPD. (2014). *HR: Getting smart about agile working.* https://www. cipd.co.uk/Images/hr-getting-smart-agile-working_2014_tcm18-14105. pdf. Accessed 10 August 2020.
4. Clement, J. (2020, June 4). *Worldwide digital population.* Statista. https://www.statista.com/statistics/617136/digital-population-worldw ide/. Accessed 10 August 2020.
5. Cooper, C. D., & Kurland, N. B. (2002). Telecommuting, professional isolation, and employee development in public and private organizations. *Journal of Organizational Behavior, 23*(4), 511–532. https://doi.org/10. 1002/job.145.
6. Elsbach, K. D., & Hargadon, A. B. (2006). Enhancing creativity through "mindless" work: A framework of workday design. *Organization Science, 17*(4), 470–483.
7. European Risk Observatory. (2014). *Calculating the costs of work-related stress and psychosocial risks.* https://osha.europa.eu/en/publications/litera ture_reviews/calculating-the-cost-of-work-related-stress-and-psychosocial-risks. Accessed 10 August 2020.
8. Golden, T. D., Veiga, J. F., & Dino, R. N. (2008). The impact of professional isolation on teleworker job performance and turnover intentions: Does time spent teleworking, interacting face-to-face, or having access to communication-enhancing technology matter? *Journal of Applied Psychology, 93*(6), 1412–1421. https://doi.org/10.1037/a0012722.
9. Grant, C. A., Wallace, L. M., & Spurgeon, P. C. (2013). An exploration of the psychological factors affecting remote e-worker's job effectiveness, well-being and work-life balance. *Employee Relations, 35*(5), 527–546. https:// doi.org/10.1108/ER-08-2012-0059.

10. Hoch, J. E., & Kozlowski, S. W. (2014). Leading virtual teams: Hierarchical leadership, structural supports, and shared team leadership. *Journal of Applied Psychology, 99*(3), 390–403. https://doi.org/10.1037/a0030264.
11. Jeyasingham, D. (2016). Open spaces, supple bodies? Considering the impact of agile working on social work office practices. *Child and Family Social Work, 21*(2), 209–217. https://doi.org/10.1111/cfs.12130.
12. Jimenez, A., Boehe, D. M., Taras, V., & Caprar, D. V. (2017). Working across boundaries: Current and future perspectives on global virtual teams. *Journal of International Management, 23*(4), 341–349. https://doi.org/10.1016/j.intman.2017.05.001.
13. Kalleberg, A. L. (2009). Precarious work, insecure workers: Employment relations in transition. *American Sociological Review, 74*(1), 1–22. https://doi.org/10.1177/000312240907400101.
14. Kelliher, C., & Anderson, D. (2010). Doing more with less? Flexible working practices and the intensification of work. *Human Relations, 63*(1), 83–106. https://doi.org/10.1177/0018726709349199.
15. McDonald, P., Bradley, L., & Brown, K. (2008). Visibility in the workplace: Still an essential ingredient for career success? *The International Journal of Human Resource Management, 19*(12), 2198–2215. https://doi.org/10.1080/09585190802479447.
16. Meier, L. L., & Gross, S. (2015). Episodes of incivility between subordinates and supervisors: Examining the role of self-control and time with an interaction-record diary study. *Journal of Organizational Behavior, 36*(8), 1096–1113. https://doi.org/10.1002/job.2013.
17. Quick, J. C., Macik-Frey, M., & Cooper, C. L. (2007). Managerial dimensions of organizational health: The healthy leader at work. *Journal of Management Studies, 44*(2), 189–205. https://doi.org/10.1111/j.1467-6486.2007.00684.x.
18. Rigby, D. K., Sutherland, J., & Takeuchi, H. (2016, May). Embracing agile. *Harvard Business Review.* https://hbr.org/2016/05/embracing-agile.
19. Russell, E., Jackson T. W., & Banks, A. P. (2019). Classifying computer-mediated communication (cmc) interruptions at work using control as a key delineator, *Behavior and Information Technology (Online only)*, 1–15. https://doi.org/10.1080/0144929X.2019.1683606.
20. Ryan, R. M., & Deci, E. L. (2001). On happiness and human potentials: A review of research on hedonic and eudemonic well-being. *Annual Review of Psychology, 52*(1), 141–166. https://doi.org/10.1146/annurev.psych.52.1.141.
21. Schlachter, S., McDowall, A., Cropley, M., & Inceoglu, I. (2018). Voluntary work-related technology use during non-work time: A narrative synthesis of empirical research and research agenda. *International Journal of Management Reviews, 20*(4), 825–846. https://doi.org/10.1111/ijmr.12165.

22. Sonnentag, S., Binnewies, C., & Mojza, E. J. (2008). " Did you have a nice evening?" A day-level study on recovery experiences, sleep, and affect. *Journal of Applied Psychology, 93*(3), 674–684. https://doi.org/10.1037/0021-9010.93.3.674.
23. Taskin, L., & Bridoux, F. (2010). Telework: a challenge to knowledge transfer in organizations. *The International Journal of Human Resource Management, 21*(13), 2503–2520. https://doi.org/10.1080/09585192.2010.516600.
24. The Agile Organization. (2010). *What is agile working?* https://www.agile.org.uk/what-is-agile-working/. Accessed 10 August 2020.
25. The Work Foundation. (2018). *Productivity technology and working anywhere.* https://www.lancaster.ac.uk/media/lancaster-university/content-assets/documents/lums/work-foundation/423_TechnologyProductivityWorkingAnywhere-updated-2-MO(1).pdf. Accessed 10 August 2020.
26. Tremblay, M. S., Colley, R. C., Saunders, T. J., Healy, G. N., & Owen, N. (2010). Physiological and health implications of a sedentary lifestyle. *Applied Physiology, Nutrition and Metabolism, 35*(6), 725–740. https://doi.org/10.1139/h10-079.
27. Wang, J., Cheng, G. H. L., Chen, T., & Leung, K. (2019). Team creativity/innovation in culturally diverse teams: A meta-analysis. *Journal of Organizational Behavior, 40*(6), 693–708. https://doi.org/10.1002/job.2362.
28. Warr, P. (1978). A study of psychological well-being. *British Journal of Psychology, 69*(1), 111–121. https://doi.org/10.1111/j.2044-8295.1978.tb01638.x.

CHAPTER 2

Concepts, Terms and Measurement in Agile Working

Christine Grant

Abstract This chapter reviews the current definitions of agile working and how previous terminology has evolved to categorise this new approach to work. The chapter explores how 'agile' working practices have emerged, through promoting flexibility, integrating resources, engaging in innovative activities and utilising new technology. The need for organisations to react to and deliver change within evolving work environments and fast-paced markets, in order to satisfy customer, organisational, market and worker needs, is considered. Further, the measurement of agile working is not common practice and there are few validated scales that capture or 'quantify' agile work and how it meets the needs of organisations. The recent development of the E-Work Life scale and sister measure, the E-Work Well-being Scale provide new and useful insights into how to measure key agile working practices relating to remote e-workers (as a 'type' of agile worker). The chapter discusses how measures

C. Grant (✉)
School of Psychological, Social and Behavioural Sciences,
Coventry University, Coventry, UK
e-mail: christine.grant@coventry.ac.uk

© The Author(s), under exclusive license to
Springer Nature Switzerland AG 2020
C. Grant and E. Russell (eds.), *Agile Working and Well-Being
in the Digital Age*, https://doi.org/10.1007/978-3-030-60283-3_2

such as these can lead to the creation of supportive strategies to optimise agile working.

Keywords Agile working · Agile work · Agile worker · Teleworking · Remote e-working · Measures · E-working scales

2.1   INTRODUCTION

This chapter provides an analysis of the related terms used within the research literature to conceptualise various practices of 'agile working'. As outlined in the Introduction chapter, the authors' comprehensive, human-focused definition for agile working involves four activities [22] focussed on: temporal and spatial flexibility, integrating resources, engaging in innovative activity and utilising information and digital technologies. These activities should always be considered in terms of the extent to which they meet the central purpose of agile working, to meet personal and organisational goals whilst responding to market, customer and service needs.

The term 'agile working' has been used in several different contexts, including and emerging from a work process used frequently in software development, which represents a project management approach implemented to effect change. More recently, the term 'agile working' has been adopted by organisations and interspersed descriptions of new forms of remote working. These work forms (e.g. teleworking, telecommuting, home working) are related to agile working in that they describe autonomous work, usually enabled by technology, that takes place at any location and at any time. Such forms of work, therefore, specifically refer to activities (i) and (iv) in our agile working definition. It is noteworthy that many of the terms that recognise different modes of working could be submerged into definitions of 'agile working', though in and of themselves do not constitute fully agile work. As such, we might argue that telecommuting or flexible working hours might indicate a form of agile working practice but are not proxies of full agile working, which involves all four activities with the purpose of meeting worker, organisation, customer and market needs.

In this chapter, it is acknowledged that many terms used to refer to agile working do not encapsulate all activities in agile working. Nevertheless, key aspects of agile working practices discussed in this chapter include flexitime and remote e-working, autonomous work and a technology-focused environment that uses innovations to support customers and service delivery. Further, in this chapter, the related history and subsequent development of the term 'agile working' are explored, along with its key features, in order to provide a comprehensive understanding of how agile working terminology is interpreted today.

This chapter will also cover the measurement of 'agile working'; notably, there are very few scales that attempt to quantify or calibrate aspects of agile working. However, measures related to a new and related phenomenon of technostress have emerged. The analysis of current measures in the field will include the author's own research and development into new scales of E-Work Life and E-Work Well-being. These scales measure the impact of technology on remote e-workers and their well-being. The purpose of this examination is to consider how such scales can support both academics and organisations in measuring elements of agile working, as a starting point for improving understanding and practice.

2.2   Terms Used in 'Agile Working'

The term 'Agile working' was first mentioned in the academic literature in the early 1990s, relating to an 'ever-changing' work environment that needed to respond to customer demands [6, 12]. To meet the fast-paced changing needs of customers, organisations began to consider how work could be structured and delivered differently [13]. Alongside the impetus to ensure that organisations were customer-focused and competitive, there was a growing need to become operationally 'lean'. This involved streamlining work processes through use of technology with a clear focus on economic viability. In this climate, fast progress in developing information and communication technologies (ICTs), to support more remote e-working, provided a means to enable work that could be flexible in time and space [26]. For organisations, this meant examining how resources could be deployed in more effective ways by changing working practices [5].

The technology industry concurrently utilised the term 'agile' in relation to software development, as outlined in the 'Agile Manifesto', which stipulated four core values that prioritised: '(i) individuals and interactions over processes and tools; (ii) working software over comprehensive documentation; (iii) customer collaboration over contract negotiation; (iv) responding to change over following a plan' [18, n.p.]. These values focus on working collaboratively with the customer and responding to change using flexible but structured processes. Related to this are 12 principles that focus on creating a work environment to respond quickly to customer needs and expectations [18]. It can be seen, therefore, that some aspects of the terminology taken from the technology industry's understanding of 'agile working' have been transferred to the notion of 'agile working' in human (i.e. organisational, human resources and applied psychology) domains. In particular, the notion that agile working supports an expeditious approach to change and to meet market and client needs, and allows employees to use technology to work efficiently and autonomously, was born from this tradition [12].

Agile working has, in more recent times, been seen as a dynamic way of working, using technology, to achieve core work goals with minimum constraints. The implications of this have been to make work possible in any location and at any time and to ensure that the organisation can not only survive, but thrive, under sometimes difficult economic challenges [12]. Agile working practices have also allowed employees the ability to integrate their personal and work needs. A definition of agile working that encapsulates the aforementioned features is outlined below and reflects the need for workers to have increased freedom of where they work by using ICTs effectively:

> *Agile working is a way of working in which an organisation empowers its people to work where, when and how they choose. Agile working combines maximum flexibility and minimum constraints to optimise performance and deliver best in class value and customer service. Using communications and information technology to enable people to work in ways that best suit their needs agile working overcomes the traditional limitations of where and when tasks must be performed.* [9, n.p.]

However, this definition does not refer to the 'innovation' involved in agile working, and nor does it consider how resources may be integrated into different ways to allow such work to happen (as per activities (ii) and (iii)—see Chapter 1). Unpacking the term 'agile working' also involves doing work differently by focusing on performance and outcomes as opposed to inputs: 'agile work is more than working in a different way, it is being and behaving differently. It is transformational' [24, n.p.]. The need to feel valued by their employers focusing on continual training and upskilling [17], given the high need to network, and to be autonomous may support innovation in agile workers. As such, the definition of agile working [22] that we present in our Introduction of this book incorporates the key elements discussed above and positions these within an organisational (rather than purely technological) context.

2.2.1   The Impetus and History Behind Remote and Flexible Working and How This Relates to 'Agile Working'

As mentioned, there are several terms that have arisen from different 'agile' working practices. Predominant in the extant literature are terms relating to teleworking, telecommuting, e-working, location independent working, home working, remote e-working and, more recently, mobile working. The terms relating to teleworking/telecommuting are generally North American in origin, whilst home working, remote e-working and other derivatives of these have developed across Europe [3, 14]. All of these terms relate to:

> the ability to work flexibly using remote technology to communicate with the workplace. [15, p. 17]

Flexible working patterns have been in use since the 1980s, when organisations began allowing staff to adopt differing working hours to suit both their needs and those of the organisation. The most popular flexible working practices included: part-time working, flexitime, job-sharing, term-time working, staggered hours, annualised hours, compressed working hours and shift-working [5]. Today, these different approaches to work are now supported by government legislation in the United Kingdom (all workers have the right to request flexible working arrangements from their employer) [11]. Whilst technology can be a liberator, it can also inhibit work recovery, especially when it is used across work-home boundaries. This is a concern given the focus on employee well-being that has driven changes in the design of work in the twenty-first century [19]. Flexible work practices, therefore, have both advantages and disadvantages. As outlined in a recent research study [14], it was noted that not all aspects of remote e-working are positive, including a lack of recuperation and separation from work, and being constantly connected; these are elucidated further in Chapter 7.

Eurofound, in their report on 'Working anytime, anywhere: The effects on the World of Work' [10], found differences in remote working

Table 2.1 Comparing the four activities of agile working related to similar terminology

Working practice	Flexible working	Telecommuting/Teleworking	Remote e-working	Agile working
(i) Promoting temporal and spatial flexibility	Working hours may or may not be spent working from home or in the office. Work times flexible across the day, providing core hours to work are mutually agreed. This gives flexibility to both the employee and the employer. Usually has clear boundaries of work and non-work time	Work times usually relate to the 'normal' working day but can vary with agreement with employer. Usually has clear boundaries of work time but can be flexible.	Autonomous, space and time are less relevant in that the worker responds to work requirements as needed, so no specific temporal parameters set by the organisation, except to be available for work when required. Boundaryless in most cases, it is up to the individual worker to set these so that personal time can be achieved	Autonomous, space and time are less relevant in that the worker responds to work requirements as needed, so no specific temporal parameters set by the organisation, except to be available for work when required. Boundaryless in most cases, it is up to the individual agile worker to set these so that personal time can be achieved
(ii) Integrating resources	Allows the employee to change between work-based and home-based working. Use of the home as an additional resource to continue working flexibly. Minimal integration	Use of the home as a work-based resource. Static environment with access to remote working through VPN to work with colleagues. Some integration with resources available	Allows for working in various different locations, including on- and off-site, with clients, meeting customer and organisational needs. People and technology become more integrated	Allows for individuals and teams to be created and dispersed as needed related to client needs. Resources are fully integrated including co-working and networking within and across organisations. Individuals can work at any time and any place using technology

Working practice	Flexible working	Telecommuting/Teleworking	Remote e-working	Agile working
(iii) Engaging in innovative activities	Flexible working can be considered to some extent as innovative as it allows working from a different location and has provided employees and employers with many benefits, e.g. retaining staff	Telecommuting similar to home working was innovative at the time and made good use of remote technology to work	Remote e-working allows greater flexibility in working times and also autonomy. Communication channels are utilised effectively to work with colleagues to meet work objectives, network and socialise	High technical capability of staff, using technology to enhance flexibility to customers (and themselves). Work in multiple locations and across different IT platforms. Communication channels are key with a wide variety incorporated into everyday working to ensure productivity is high and goals met
(iv) Utilising new communication and digital technologies	Technology to be available in work and at home, linked to the organisation's VPN for home working. Sometimes requires use of own computer equipment	Technology to be available in work and at home, linked to the organisation's VPN for home working. Sometimes requires use of own computer equipment	Technology supplied by employer, usually for use at various locations including work, home, off-site with clients, etc., Linked to the organisation's VPN and other networks	Use of own or work purchased technology. High specification of technology for working across multiple locations. Continual link to organisational VPN

practices and considered that there are four types of remote worker, cate-gorised in terms of the degree to which they e-work. These types include: (i) those who are regularly home-based using ICTs to support their work; (ii) those who are highly mobile, regularly working remotely in several locations with high ICT usage and skill; (iii) those who occasionally work in one or more places outside of the employer's premises but with lower mobility using ICTs; and iv) those who are constantly connected on the employers' premises, with or without ICTs [10]. This highlights the way in which agile working can be interpreted and undertaken according to individual preferences and organisational requirements.

Table 2.1 uses the four areas from the definition of agile working [22] to compare the components of agile working against the differing terms used to describe similar way of working.

2.3   MEASUREMENT OF AGILE WORKING

At the time of writing, there is no current validated measure of agile working that covers each of the four activities described above, meaning that the extent to which one is involved in agile working requires a subjective 'count' or appraisal of how many of the four activities are engaged. However, some aspects or repercussions of agile working prac-tices have been measured both academically and by organisations seeking to consider the impact of agile working on outcomes, such as work-life balance. For example, surveys of remote workers have included measures of work-family conflict (an agile working outcome) [1, 8, 23]. In one study of work-life balance [20], over 1500 teleworkers completed 150 questions on a range of outputs associated with teleworking, including working hours, travel, job performance, motivation and satisfaction. Find-ings indicated that 'controlling working hours' [20, p. 76] was the most important activity for promoting work-life balance. In these early studies, it can be seen that the focus was on measuring flexible working practices and how this impacted outcomes like work-life balance. More recently, there have been studies attempting to measure the phenomenon of 'technostress', which examines aspects of work pressure and motivation associated with constantly using technology [7, 16]. These studies have found high levels of stress related to technology use.

Whilst these types of measures are important, they do not provide a single holistic measure of the multiple facets of agile working activity and outputs, including work effectiveness, goal achievement, work-life balance and well-being. Measures and surveys in this area only usually focus on one activity, e.g. remote working or technology use. Furthermore, existing scales or surveys rarely measure multiple levels associated with agile work, i.e. micro-levels (individual experiences), dyadic (individual-supervisor experiences) and macro-levels (organisational/societal experiences). Another aspect that has been missing from current scales is that they are not 'actionable'; that is, they do not have strategies that are specifically aligned to the scale outcomes.

2.3.1   *The E-Work Life Scale*

To fill this gap in the research, a new scale was developed that could measure multiple consequences of remote e-working including work-life balance, well-being and job effectiveness. This scale is the E-Work Life scale (EWL) [15]. The E-Work Life scale was developed in response to the lack of a comprehensive measure in this area and because of the increase in remote e-working related to the increase in technology access [14]. To devise the EWL scale, a review of the literature pertaining to remote e-working and related measures in the field was completed, followed by a qualitative study of the psychological experiences of current e-workers [3]. This scale was developed as a composite measure of remote e-working in relation to: (i) e-working effectiveness, (ii) e-job effectiveness, (iii) management style, (iv) trust, (v) e-well-being, (vi) work-life integration, (vii) role management/conflict and (viii) managing boundaries. The scale provides a means for individuals, managers and organisations to assess remote e-workers and consider what interventions and strategies may be effective to support e-workers to experience more positive outcomes. The scale has been tested using a wide-scale survey of remote e-workers, across 11 organisations, 3 sectors and multiple job roles. A 4-factor structure was confirmed grouping together the facets and measuring: Work-Life Interference; Productivity and Effectiveness; Organisational Trust; and Flexibility, and it was found to be valid with good reliability [15]. This research produced a theoretically reliable measure of multiple dimensions of remote e-working.

Further to the EWL scale, a new sister scale was developed to specifically focus on the well-being of remote e-workers, the E-Work Well-being measure [2]. This measure is based on Van Horn's theoretical model of well-being, focusing on five dimensions: (i) cognitive weariness; (ii) social relationships, including isolation; (iii) affective emotion, including attachment to work (job satisfaction and engagement); (iv) physical complaints; and (v) professionalism, related to autonomy and career progression [25]. This measure goes beyond early and singular measures of technostress by providing a multifaceted approach to measuring remote e-workers' well-being. These two measures are an important development in the measurement of agile working practices. With organisations swiftly moving to remote e-working, to increase their flexibility in responding to both worker needs, market and environmental conditions, there is a dearth of measurement to uncover the extent to which e-workers are working effectively and experiencing work-life balance and well-being. Both the EWL and EWW scales provide a partial solution to the measurement gaps in agile working research. The scales address previously unexplored areas of remote e-working, including the psychological aspects of working remotely and the associated well-being of an increasingly agile population.

2.4   Future Directions in Agile Working

Organisations today need to both instigate and respond to frequent and considerable change in order to stay ahead of both market/service/customer conditions, and a changing workforce. In reference to this, the global COVID-19 pandemic that impacted working life in 2019–2020 demonstrated just how important it was that organisations could promote and encourage agile working practices. Indeed, as part of the pandemic situation, many organisations immediately required large sections of workforce to become more agile in their working practices; for many, this meant remote e-working for the first time (see Chapters 1 and 12). This has raised issues for a new population of remote e-workers and their organisations, including how to manage staff well-being remotely and ensure productivity continues, without inducing staff burnout. For organisations that could facilitate a move to agile working, the pandemic escalated concerns about how to effectively remote e-work. It also demonstrated how quickly organisations can change to a different mode of working, if the need arises.

Whilst specific measures of agile working are in short supply, surveys that explore evolving working practices are more popular. The Chartered Institute of Personnel and Development (CIPD) [4] reported on agile working practices from a large sample of HR leaders and employees, across a range of job roles and sectors. They found that the 'norm of where people work is changing…, with only 45% of employees saying they work from the company's core office most of the time, and 64% staying at the same desk most of the time. Only 7% work from home most of the time (and 51% never work from home), although the same is true of 22% of employees in 'nonstandard' jobs' [19, pp. 6–7]. Agile working, therefore, is likely to continue to grow, with a focus on working different locations in which to work, co-working and community hubs are likely to emerge (see Chapter 12).

Organisations are also observing Millennials starting to forge and demand new ways of working. As digital natives, they are able to work more flexibly and want equal consideration for both their working and non-working lives [21]. It is likely that this generation will reshape the way we work, agile working with greater ease than the previous generation but perhaps with different issues related to their well-being and additional requirements for knowledge, skills and attitudes to be developed as agile workers.

2.5   CONCLUSION

In this chapter, we noted how terminology for remote e-working (and related terms such as teleworking and home working) has captured key activities of agile working, specifically relating to flexibility and use of technology to transcend time and space boundaries. Agile working allows individuals and organisations to manage their time effectively ensuring that work can be completed in multiple locations and across geographical time zones. Clarity in definitions between the different styles of remote e-working is important; being an effective agile worker requires the worker to be able to manage both multiple locations of work but also time, creating their own boundaries and communicating effectively to a number of colleagues/clients and managers. However, it is clear that a focus on modes of working that support *all* agile working activities, including the embracing of innovation and integration of resources, is now needed. In addition, researchers need to apply a robust measurement of agile working to support worker well-being. There is a shortage of appropriate measures for agile working. However, with the newly developed E-Work Life and E-Work Well-being scales, we can begin to assess how individual agile workers and their managers are coping with changing work practices.

Outcomes of these measures can then be used to inform the development of organisational policy and guidance, thus creating appropriate and supportive well-being culture for agile workers.

REFERENCES

1. Baruch, Y. (2000). Teleworking: Benefits and pitfalls as perceived by professionals and managers. *New Technology, Work and Employment, 15*(1), 34–49. https://doi.org/10.1111/1468-005X.00063.
2. Charalampous, M. (2020). *The development of the e-well-being scale and further validation of the e-work Life scale.* Unpublished PhD Thesis. Coventry University.
3. Charalampous, M., Grant, C. A., Tramontano, C., & Michailidis, E. (2019). Systematically reviewing remote e-workers' well-being at work: A multi-dimensional approach. *Journal of European Work and Organisational Psychology, 28*(1), 51–73. https://doi.org/10.1080/1359432X.2018.1541886.
4. CIPD. (2014). *HR: Getting smart about agile working.* https://www.cipd.co.uk/Images/hr-getting-smart-agile-working 2014 tcm18-14105.pdf. Accessed 2 March 2020.
5. Clarke, S., & Holdsworth, L. (2017). *Flexibility in the workplace: Implications of flexible work arrangements for individuals, teams and organisations. ACAS.* https://archive.acas.org.uk/media/4901/Flexibility-in-the-Workplace-Implications-of-flexible-work-arrangements-for-individuals-teams-and-organisations/pdf/Flexibility-in-the-Workplace.pdf. Accessed 17 April 2020.
6. Davenport, T. H., Jarvenpaa, S. L., & Beers, M. C. (1996). Improving knowledge work processes. *Sloan Management Review, 37*(4), 53–65.
7. Derks, D., Duin, D., Tims, M., & Bakker, A. B. (2015). Smartphone use and work–home interference: The moderating role of social norms and employee work engagement. *Journal of Occupational and Organizational Psychology, 88*(1), 155–177. https://doi.org/10.1111/joop.12083.
8. Duxbury, L. E., Higgins, C. A., & Mills, S. (1992). After-hours telecommuting and work-family conflict: A comparative analysis. *Information Systems Research, 3*(2), 173–190. https://doi.org/10.1287/isre.3.2.173.
9. Employer Network for Equality and Inclusion. Agile working: *A guide for Employers. Employer Network for Equality for Equality and Diversity* https://www.enei.org.uk/diversity-inclusion/excellence-in-diversity-inclusion/agile-working/. Accessed 13 April 2020.
10. Eurofound and the International Labour Office (2017). *Working anytime, anywhere: The effects on the world of work.* Publications Office of the European Union, Luxembourg, and the International Labour Office, Geneva. http://eurofound.link/ef1658. Accessed 2 March 2020.

11. Flexible working guidance. https://www.gov.uk/flexible-working. Accessed 17 April 2020.
12. Gillies, D. (2011). Agile bodies: A new imperative in neoliberal governance. *Journal of Education Policy, 26*(2), 207–223. https://doi.org/10.1080/026 80939.2010.508177.
13. Goldman, S. L., Nagel, R. N., & Preiss, K. (1994). *Agile competitors and virtual organisations: Strategies for enriching the customer (Industrial Engineering)*. New York: Van Nostrand Reinhold.
14. Grant, C. A., Wallace, L. M., & Spurgeon, P. C. (2013). An exploration of the psychological factors affecting remote e-worker's job effectiveness, well-being and work-life balance. *Employee Relations, 35*(5), 525–546. https://doi.org/10.1108/ER-08-2012-0059.
15. Grant, C. A., Wallace, L., Spurgeon, P., Tramontano, C., & Charalampous, M. (2019). Construction and initial validation of the E-Work Life Scale to measure remote e-working. *Employee Relations, 41*(1), 16–33. https://doi.org/10.1108/ER-09-2017-0229.
16. Hung, W. H., Chang, L. M., & Lin, C. H. (2011). *Managing the risk of overusing mobile phones in the working environment: A study of ubiquitous technostress.* Proceedings of the 15th Pacific Asia Conference on Information Systems, Brisbane, Australia. https://aisel.aisnet.org/pacis2011/81/.
17. Jaysingham, S., Govindasamy, M., & Singh, S. K. G. (2016). Instilling affective commitment insights on what makes knowledge workers want to stay. *Management Research Review, 39*(3), 266–288. https://doi.org/10.1108/MRR-03-2014-0060.
18. Laanti, M., Similä J., & Abrahamsson, P. (2013). Definitions of agile software development and agility. In F. McCaffery, R. V. O'Connor, R. Messnarz (Eds.), Systems, Software and Services Process Improvement. EuroSPI 2013. *Communications in computer and information science* (pp. 247–258). Springer. https://doi.org/10.1007/978-3-642-39179-8_22. Accessed 2 March 2020.
19. Litchfield, P., Cooper, C., Hancock, C., & Watt, P. (2016). Work and well-being in the 21st century. *International Journal of Environmental Research and Public Health, 13*(11), 1065. https://doi.org/10.3390/ijerph 13111065.
20. Maruyama, T., Hopkinson, P. G., & James, P. W. (2009). A multivariate analysis of work–life balance outcomes from a large-scale telework programme. *New Technology, Work and Employment, 24*(1), 76–88. https://doi.org/10.1111/j.1468-005X.2008.00219.x.
21. PWC. (2011, April 20). *Millennials at work Reshaping the workplace.* https://www.pwc.com/co/es/publicaciones/assets/millennials-at-work.pdf. Accessed 17 April 2020.

22. Russell, E., & Grant, C. A. (2020). Chapter 1: Introduction to agile working and well-being in the digital age. In C. Grant & E. Russell (Eds.), *Agile working and well-being in the digital age* (pp. X-XX). London: Palgrave Macmillan.
23. Sullivan, C., & Lewis, S. (2001). Home-based telework, gender, and the synchronization of work and family: Perspectives of teleworkers and their co-residents. *Gender Work and Organization, 8*(2), 123–145. https://doi.org/10.1111/1468-0432.00125.
24. The Agile Organisation. *What is agile working?* https://www.agile.org.uk/what-is-agile-working/. Accessed 2 March 2020.
25. Van Horn, J. E., Taris, T. W., Schaufeli, W. B., & Schreurs, P. J. (2004). The structure of occupational well-being: A study among Dutch teachers. *Journal of Occupational and Organizational Psychology, 77*(3), 365–375. https://doi.org/10.1348/0963179041752718.
26. WBDG. (2016, May 5). *The changing nature of organizations, work, and workplace.* https://www.wbdg.org/resources/changing-nature-organizations-work-and-workplace. Accessed 17 April 2020.

PART II

Managing Boundaries

CHAPTER 3

Boundary Management: Getting the Work-Home Balance Right

Kelly A. Basile and T. Alexandra Beauregard

Abstract Agile working involves liberation from traditional ways of working, such that boundaries between work and home (both physical and temporal) can become blurred. In this chapter, we explore how boundary management preferences for integration or segmentation, and the fit between these preferences and agile working modalities, can influence experiences of the work-life interface, work-related attitudes and employee well-being. We go on to identify the challenges that agile working presents for boundary management, related to an increasingly 'always on' work culture. We conclude by discussing what organizations can do to support employees' management of work-life boundaries in pursuit of satisfactory levels of performance and well-being in each life domain.

K. A. Basile (✉)
Emmanuel College, Boston, MA, USA
e-mail: basilek@emmanuel.edu

T. A. Beauregard
Birkbeck College, University of London, London, UK
e-mail: a.beauregard@bbk.ac.uk

© The Author(s), under exclusive license to
Springer Nature Switzerland AG 2020
C. Grant and E. Russell (eds.), *Agile Working and Well-Being in the Digital Age*, https://doi.org/10.1007/978-3-030-60283-3_3

Keywords Work-life balance · Work-family conflict · Border theory · Boundary management · Integration · Segmentation

3.1   INTRODUCTION

Agile working allows employees to take control over the timing and location of their work activities. While increased control over work activities can help employees better manage their work and non-work roles, agile working can also blur the boundaries between these roles [15, 24]. For example, flexible starting and stopping times for work activities can result in employees working much later into the evening than they might with a fixed stopping time. Similarly, working from home may facilitate certain aspects of family life, but the removal of the physical boundary of an office location may result in constant reminders of and/or requests to work when engaged in non-work activities.

Boundaries are mental constructions of the dividing lines between different life domains, such as paid work, family and leisure. Managing boundaries can impact the extent to which work and personal roles conflict with or facilitate one another [1]. While research has increased substantially on the topic of boundary management over the last few decades, organisations are still struggling to find ways to support employees as they balance work and non-work roles. Central to this challenge is the impact of technology, which has enabled many organisations to espouse an 'always on' culture, such that employees feel compelled to stay 'switched on' to work and are expected to respond instantly to technology-enabled communications [29]. In addition, organisations must be responsive to the different preferences held by employees regarding the types of boundaries they negotiate between the domains of work and non-work. For example, organisational interventions to promote agile working aim to help employees integrate work and non-work responsibilities and may lead to reduced work recovery time and decreased well-being, particularly among employees who prefer to keep work and non-work activities separate [20, 24, 32].

In this chapter, we explore key theories and research that contribute to our knowledge of work-life boundary management, discussing how boundaries influence experiences of the interface between work and non-work roles. We go on to identify challenges for boundary management arising from agile working practices such as remote working in a constantly connected work culture. We conclude by identifying some best practices for agile working that organisations can use to support employees' management of work-life boundaries in pursuit of satisfactory levels of performance and well-being in each life domain.

3.2 Defining Work-Life Boundaries

Border Theory identifies three types of boundaries that individuals construct between work and non-work roles; physical, temporal and psychological [10]. Physical boundaries represent the actual spaces where work and non-work activities take place. For example, a remote e-worker might create a physical boundary in their home by having a separate room that serves as an office for work activities. Temporal boundaries use time to create borders between work and non-work activities [10], as when a worker sets a 5:00 p.m. deadline to end their working day because they need to collect their children from after-school care. Psychological boundaries are the rules that workers create regarding the emotions, behaviours and thinking patterns that might be displayed in one domain but not the other [1]. For instance, an employee may behave in a nurturing and caring manner when dealing with their children at home, but a more reserved and formal manner when dealing with colleagues at work.

The boundaries we create help us to navigate the extent to which our work and personal roles overlap. While some individuals seek to keep roles highly separate (segmentation), others prefer more overlap (integration), such that the experiences and events related to one role may frequently impact or disrupt the other [9]. These integrating/segmenting preferences span a continuum, with few individuals maintaining fully integrated or fully segmented lifestyles [32]. Some research makes a case for the benefits of work-life integration; integration can lead to work and family roles enhancing one another, such that the greater the level of integration, the greater the impact of job satisfaction on positive home affect and marital satisfaction [20]. In addition, forms of agile working that foster integration, such as remote e-work, can help to reduce work-life conflict and lead to improved well-being [13]. However, the converse can also be true; high levels of work-life integration can result in 'role blurring', which is also associated with higher levels of work-life conflict [15]. In addition, greater role integration may mean that individuals experience less recovery time from work activities leading to reduced well-being [39].

3.3   MANAGING BOUNDARIES

Individuals adopt boundary tactics that allow them to manage work and non-work roles according to their preferences for segmentation or integration. Segmenters tend to build strong boundaries between work and non-work roles, while integrators tend to have weaker boundaries that allow for frequent transitions between roles [24, 32]. Research has identified physical, behavioural, temporal and communicative strategies to strengthen the boundaries between work and personal activities [25], which are likely to be more appealing to those with a preference for segmentation. For example, remote e-workers, who favour segmentation, often recreate the physical boundary of an office environment by conducting work activities in a designated space in their home where personal or family activities do not take place. They may also make commitments to spend time with non-work colleagues, and take part in scheduled activities, in order to create a temporal boundary between working time and personal time [5]. Behavioural tactics might involve workers not checking personal email or text messages at the office, in order to keep that time focused purely on work activities [18]. Communicative tactics could also relate to setting expectations with co-workers and clients about one's hours of availability for work-related communications, in order to avoid interruption of family time [18].

The strength of boundaries between home and work roles is determined by difference in the flexibility and permeability of boundaries [3, 9]. Flexibility can be measured by the extent to which a worker is both able and willing to modify the temporal and physical restrictions of their work environment [9]. An employee who can adjust their working hours to suit their family needs has high temporal boundary flexibility-ability, but if they prefer to work a standard 9-to-5 schedule then they have low flexibility-willingness [27]. Boundary permeability can be measured by the extent to which individuals experience frequent physical or psychological transitions (or interruptions) between roles [3, 10, 27]. For example, if an employee has argued with a family member at home before work, they may experience frequent psychological interruptions in their workday, thereby increasing the permeability of the work-home boundary.

The management of permeability and flexibility is a reciprocal process. While individuals have preferences for integrating or segmenting their roles, organisations also supply resources, or make demands, that affect employees' ability to execute their boundary management preferences [15]. Organisational resources and demands are influenced by organisational culture, national culture and industry constraints [8]. For example, in societies that tend to be more collectivist, both individuals and organisations may place more emphasis on family and community well-being and therefore, offer more forms of agile/integrative work [35]. In addition, industries are often constrained in their ability to offer forms of working that suit all employee preferences. For example, manufacturing jobs typically require a physical presence in the workplace, which enforces role segmentation, while technology-based jobs may allow remote e-work that increases the integration between work and family roles. Another consideration is the distributive justice associated with levels of integration; if an organisation allows flexibility for personal responsibilities to interrupt work, to what extent might the organisation then expect that work responsibilities can cross non-work boundaries [22]?

There is no clear indication that either segmentation or integration leads to better outcomes for well-being and performance; it is the fit between an employee's preferences for integration/segmentation and their organisation's supply of integrating/segmenting policies and practices that has the greatest impact [24]. In the context of boundary management, fit occurs when organisations supply employees with environments that are congruent with their segmentation/integration preferences [24]. For example, a study of offshore workers found that misfit resulting from an oversupply of segmentation relative to employee preferences—in the form of lengthy rotations away from home, followed by long periods away from work—reduced employee well-being; in this case 'misfit' led to conflict between work and family roles and reduced employees' commitment to the organisation [6].

3.4   AGILE WORKING CHALLENGES TO BOUNDARY MANAGEMENT

Our evolving work environment presents several challenges to the management of work-life boundaries. Two central concerns are technology use that leads to a culture that is constantly connected and the significant rise in alternative ways of working including agile working practices, such as flexible work, remote work and gig work. Research has identified the paradox of technology use in organisations; technology is credited with both supporting and harming work-life boundary management [22]. Technology use can increase boundary flexibility by giving individuals greater control over working hours and location [12]. In addition, technology can be used to build and manage boundaries between work and other roles; research suggests that individuals can use technology to ring-fence non-work time, which involves actions, such as turning off technology-enabled links to work (phones, laptops) when they do not want to be interrupted, as well as to manage transitions between home and work life [17, 28]. However, technology has increased our ability to be available for and responsive to organisational needs. The more technology is used to connect to work, beyond the temporal, physical and psychological work domain, the stronger the culture of being 'always on' becomes [30]. A large body of research demonstrates that the interference of work in the home domain, created by constant availability, can (i) negatively impact work-related outcomes such as work satisfaction, organisational commitment and job performance, and, (ii) negatively impact family-related outcomes, such as marital and family satisfaction. The negative impact on individual well-being has also been shown across categories such as reduced life satisfaction, poor sleep quality, physical and mental health problems, and psychological strain [2]. In effect, technology use may be a new form of a role boundary that moderates the level of connectivity between the employee and the organisation.

Research suggests that both segmentation/integration preferences and organisational norms and expectations can play a role in how technology disrupts boundary management [34]. Preferences for segmentation and stronger workgroup 'segmentation norms' (e.g. visibility of colleagues practising segmentation) have been found to increase employees' ability to psychologically detach from work [33]. Detachment from work helps to promote recovery and increased well-being [39]. However, when segmenters face organisational expectations for after-hours work via ICT use, this incongruence between their segmentation-integration preference and their work environment can lead to lower job satisfaction and organisational commitment, and increased stress and work-life conflict [24, 34]. Similarly, there is evidence that the relationship between after-hours smartphone use and work interference is stronger among employees who perceive high supervisor expectations for after-hours availability than among employees who do not experience these expectations [11].

Compounding the impact of technology that enables constant contact with work are alternative work arrangements that blur the physical boundaries between work and personal roles. Working from home has numerous benefits; organisations see gains in employee productivity related to both extended working hours [7, 22] and reduced distractions [4] as well as positive well-being outcomes including increased employee job satisfaction, commitment, and engagement [21, 22]. For many employees, the opportunity to work from home can facilitate work-family balance through reduced commuting times [7] and improved relationships with family members [4]. However, individuals and organisations need to weigh the costs and benefits of bringing work into the home environment; research on flexible working practices demonstrates both a positive and negative impact on employee well-being [38]. Without the physical boundary of an office setting or the temporal boundary of set working hours, the unintended results of agile working may include increased role interruptions and work intensification, which can be harmful for both segmenters and integrators [22, 38]. Research on remote e-workers has identified that boundaries between work and personal roles can be more difficult to establish and maintain when the temporal and physical markers associated with in-office work are removed [31]. Self-employment and the newer models of gig work (work that is sourced and performed remotely via online platforms), may further complicate our ability to create healthy boundaries [26]. Because these practices involve increases in part-time work, work via a third-party agency and precarious contracting [37], even more complexity is created in terms of boundary management. For example, self-employed homeworkers are often 'always on' for both work and family obligations; in addition to being primary caregivers, these workers may experience increased pressure to be available 24-7 for clients in order to generate income [19].

3.5   How Can Organisations Provide Boundary Management Support?

Interventions to support boundary management during agile work must be flexible enough to accommodate individual differences, while simultaneously ensuring that the options on offer do not disrupt work performance or inhibit well-being. Organisations can consider three levels of interventions: individual, supervisory and organisational. First, organisations can attempt to design job roles that provide workers with autonomy and control over where and when work is performed. With greater autonomy, employees can pursue the level of integration or segmentation that matches their preferences. In a study of high-tech workers, agile working was associated with lower levels of work-life conflict when employees felt they had scheduling flexibility and job autonomy [16]. Further research has found that while computer-use outside of work hours does increase work-home conflict, conflict is lessened when employees perceive low organisational norms for integration [14]. This suggests that when integration is self-driven and voluntary, it may be less disruptive to employee well-being.

Next, organisations should ensure that supervisors support employee choice through their actions and communications. Supervisors who enact segmenting behaviours are more likely to be perceived as work-family friendly role models, encouraging employees (particularly segmenters) to build boundaries between home and work, resulting in less conflict, exhaustion and disengagement [23]. Supervisors also need to consider the preferences of integrators and ensure that enough flexibility is built into work schedules to allow integrators to make the necessary transitions between work and non-work roles. Finally, organisations should set clear expectations and policies related to working beyond the scope of a traditional workday. In a recent survey of UK professionals, almost 60% reported that their employers provided no guidance on managing technology use outside of traditional work boundaries [29]. This is worrying when the distribution of work extendable technologies has been found to increase the likelihood that employees engage in work activities during personal time [36]. The adoption of clear and consistent organisational guidance related to technology use and expectations of availability may give workers more clarity and reduce anxiety associated with the need to feel 'always on', and thereby improve satisfaction with the balance between work and family roles.

3.6   CONCLUSION

This chapter has reviewed research on work-life boundaries and boundary management practices to better understand the challenges faced and support needed by agile workers. Drawing on Border and 'Fit' theories, this chapter identifies important considerations for agile worker boundary management, including; individual preferences, institutional and cultural constraints and demands, and organisational justice. In particular, the role technology plays in building and disrupting boundary strategies was highlighted. This chapter also identifies individual, supervisory and organisational interventions which can facilitate the ability of agile workers to construct healthy work-life boundaries that match their preferences. Greater recognition for the importance of supporting agile workers in the construction of healthy work/home boundaries will help to facilitate more positive work and home outcomes.

REFERENCES

1. Allen, T. D., Cho, E., & Meier, L. L. (2014). Work–family boundary dynamics. *Annual Review of Organizational Psychology and Organizational Behavior, 1*(1), 99–121. https://doi.org/10.1146/annurev-orgpsych-031413-091330.
2. Amstad, F. T., Meier, L. L., Fasel, U., Elfering, A., & Semmer, N. K. (2011). A meta-analysis of work–family conflict and various outcomes with a special emphasis on cross-domain versus matching-domain relations. *Journal of Occupational Health Psychology, 16*(2), 151–169. https://doi.org/10.1037/a0022170.
3. Ashforth, B. E., Kreiner, G. E., & Fugate, M. (2000). All in a day's work: Boundaries and micro role transitions. *Academy of Management Review, 25*(3), 472–491. https://doi.org/10.2307/259305.
4. Baruch, Y. (2000). Teleworking: benefits and pitfalls as perceived by professionals and managers. *New Technology, Work and Employment, 15*(1), 34–49. https://doi.org/10.1111/1468-005X.00063.
5. Basile, K. A., & Beauregard, T. A. (2016). Strategies for successful telework: How effective employees manage work/home boundaries. *Strategic HR Review, 15*(3), 106–111. https://doi.org/10.1108/SHR-03-2016-0024.
6. Basile, K. A., & Beauregard, T. A. (2018). Oceans apart: Work-life boundaries and the effects of an oversupply of segmentation. *International Journal of Human Resource Management*, 1–32. (Online only). https://doi.org/10.1080/09585192.2018.1512513.
7. Beauregard, T. A., Basile, K. A., & Canónico, E. (2013). *Home is where the work is: A new study of homeworking in Acas—And beyond.* ACAS Research Paper. https://archive.acas.org.uk/media/3898/Home-is-where-the-work-is-A-new-study-of-homeworking-in-Acas–and-beyond/pdf/Home-is-where-the-work-is-a-new-study-of-homeworking-in-Acas_and-beyond.pdf. Accessed 10 August 2020.
8. Beauregard, T. A., Basile, K. A., & Thompson, C. A. (2018). Organizational culture in the context of national culture. In R. Johnson, W. Shen, & K. M.

Shockley (Eds.), *The Cambridge handbook of the global work-family interface* (pp. 555–569). Cambridge: Cambridge University Press.

9. Bulger, C. A., Matthews, R. A., & Hoffman, M. E. (2007). Work and personal life boundary management: Boundary strength, work/personal life balance, and the segmentation-integration continuum. *Journal of Occupational Health Psychology, 12*(4), 365–375. https://doi.org/10.1037/1076-8998.12.4.365.

10. Clark, S. C. (2000). Work/family border theory: A new theory of work/family balance. *Human Relations, 53*(6), 747–770. https://doi.org/10.1177/0018726700536001.

11. Derks, D., Duin, D., Tims, M., & Bakker, A. B. (2015). Smartphone use and work–home interference: The moderating role of social norms and employee work engagement. *Journal of Occupational and Organizational Psychology, 88*(1), 155–177. https://doi.org/10.1111/joop.12083.

12. Diaz, I., Chiaburu, D. S., Zimmerman, R. D., & Boswell, W. R. (2012). Communication technology: Pros and cons of constant connection to work. *Journal of Vocational Behavior, 80*(2), 500–508. https://doi.org/10.1016/j.jvb.2011.08.007.

13. Fonner, K. L., & Roloff, M. E. (2010). Why teleworkers are more satisfied with their jobs than are office-based workers: When less contact is beneficial. *Journal of Applied Communication Research, 38*(4), 336–361. https://doi.org/10.1080/00909882.2010.513998.

14. Gadeyne, N., Verbruggen, M., Delanoeije, J., & De Cooman, R. (2018). All wired, all tired? Work-related ICT-use outside work hours and work-to-home conflict: The role of integration preference, integration norms and work demands. *Journal of Vocational Behavior, 107*, 86–99. https://doi.org/10.1016/j.jvb.2018.03.008.

15. Glavin, P., & Schieman, S. (2012). Work–family role blurring and work–family conflict: The moderating influence of job resources and job demands. *Work and Occupations, 39*(1), 71–98. https://doi.org/10.1177/0730888411406295.

16. Golden, T. D. (2006). The role of relationships in understanding telecommuter satisfaction. *Journal of Organizational Behavior, 27*(3), 319–340. https://doi.org/10.1002/job.369.

17. Golden, A. G., & Geisler, C. (2007). Work–life boundary management and the personal digital assistant. *Human Relations, 60*(3), 519–551. https://doi.org/10.1177/0018726707076698.

18. Greenhaus, J. H., & Beutell, N. J. (1985). Sources of conflict between work and family roles. *Academy of Management Review, 10*(1), 76–88. https://doi.org/10.2307/258214.

19. Hilbrecht, M., & Lero, D. S. (2014). Self-employment and family life: Constructing work–life balance when you're 'always on'. *Community,*

Work & Family, *17*(1), 20–42. https://doi.org/10.1080/13668803.2013. 862214.

20. Ilies, R., Wilson, K. S., & Wagner, D. T. (2009). The spillover of daily job satisfaction onto employees' family lives: The facilitating role of work-family integration. *Academy of Management Journal*, *52*(1), 87–102. https://doi.org/10.5465/AMJ.2009.36461938.

21. Kelliher, C., & Anderson, D. (2008). For better or for worse? An analysis of how flexible working practices influence employees' perceptions of job quality. *International Journal of Human Resource Management*, *19*(3), 419–431. https://doi.org/10.1080/09585190801895502.

22. Kelliher, C., & Anderson, D. (2010). Doing more with less? Flexible working practices and the intensification of work. *Human Relations*, *63*(1), 83–106. https://doi.org/10.1177/0018726709349199.

23. Koch, A. R., & Binnewies, C. (2015). Setting a good example: Supervisors as work-life-friendly role models within the context of boundary management. *Journal of Occupational Health Psychology*, *20*(1), 82–92. https://psycnet.apa.org/doi/10.1037/a0037890.

24. Kreiner, G. E. (2006). Consequences of work-home segmentation or integration: A person-environment fit perspective. *Journal of Organizational Behavior*, *27*(4), 485–507. https://doi.org/10.1002/job.386.

25. Kreiner, G. E., Hollensbe, E. C., & Sheep, M. L. (2009). Balancing borders and bridges: Negotiating the work-home interface via boundary work tactics. *Academy of Management Journal*, *52*(4), 704–730. https://doi.org/10.5465/amj.2009.43669916.

26. Lehdonvirta, V. (2018). Flexibility in the gig economy: managing time on three online piecework platforms. *New Technology, Work and Employment*, *33*(1), 13–29. https://doi.org/10.1111/ntwe.12102.

27. Matthews, R. A., Barnes-Farrell, J. L., & Bulger, C. A. (2010). Advancing measurement of work and family domain boundary characteristics. *Journal of Vocational Behavior*, *77*(3), 447–460. https://doi.org/10.1016/j.jvb.2010.05.008.

28. Matusik, S. F., & Mickel, A. E. (2011). Embracing or embattled by converged mobile devices? Users' experiences with a contemporary connectivity technology. *Human Relations*, *64*(8), 1001–1030. https://doi.org/10.1177/0018726711405552.

29. McDowall, A., & Kinman, G. (2017). The new nowhere land? A research and practice agenda for the "always on" culture. *Journal of Organizational Effectiveness: People and Performance*, *4*(3), 256–266. https://doi.org/10.1108/JOEPP-05-2017-0045.

30. Middleton, C. A. (2007). Illusions of balance and control in an always-on environment: A case study of BlackBerry users. *Continuum*, *21*(2), 165–178. https://doi.org/10.1080/10304310701268695.

31. Mustafa, M., & Gold, M. (2013). 'Chained to my work'? Strategies to manage temporal and physical boundaries among self-employed teleworkers. *Human Resource Management Journal, 23*(4), 413–429. https://doi.org/10.1111/1748-8583.12009.
32. Nippert-Eng, C. (1996). *Home and work: Negotiating boundaries through everyday life.* Chicago, IL: University of Chicago Press.
33. Park, Y., Fritz, C., & Jex, S. M. (2011). Relationships between work-home segmentation and psychological detachment from work: The role of communication technology use at home. *Journal of Occupational Health Psychology, 16*(4), 457–467.
34. Piszczek, M. M. (2017). Boundary control and controlled boundaries: Organizational expectations for technology use at the work–family interface. *Journal of Organizational Behavior, 38*(4), 592–611. https://doi.org/10.1002/job.2153.
35. Powell, G. N., Francesco, A. M., & Ling, Y. (2009). Toward culture-sensitive theories of the work–family interface. *Journal of Organizational Behavior, 30*(5), 597–616. https://doi.org/10.1002/job.568.
36. Richardson, K., & Benbunan-Fich, R. (2011). Examining the antecedents of work connectivity behavior during non-work time. *Information and Organization, 21*(3), 142–160. https://doi.org/10.1016/j.infoandorg.2011.06.002.
37. Spreitzer, G. M., Cameron, L., & Garrett, L. (2017). Alternative work arrangements: Two images of the new world of work. *Annual Review of Organizational Psychology and Organizational Behavior, 4*, 473–499. https://doi.org/10.1146/annurev-orgpsych-032516-113332.
38. ter Hoeven, C. L., & van Zoonen, W. (2015). Flexible work designs and employee well-being: Examining the effects of resources and demands. *New Technology, Work and Employment, 30*(3), 237–255. https://doi.org/10.1111/ntwe.12052.
39. Wepfer, A. G., Allen, T. D., Brauchli, R., Jenny, G. J., & Bauer, G. F. (2018). Work-life boundaries and well-being: does work-to-life integration impair well-being through lack of recovery? *Journal of Business and Psychology, 33*(6), 727–740. https://doi.org/10.1007/s10869-017-9520-y.

PART III

Managing Digital Communications

CHAPTER 4

The Paradox of Work-Email: Individual Differences in Agile Digital Work

Emma Russell

Abstract Agile working practices involve connecting with new technologies in order to operate more flexibly, efficiently and responsively. Electronic mail (or email) is one technology that particularly enables this, owing to its anywhere, anytime, anyplace functionality. However, there is a paradox in the way that workers use work-email, with research reporting as many benefits as drawbacks to this ubiquitous tool. In this chapter, it is suggested that individual differences in personality, resources and goal-preferences can explain why such a paradox has emerged, and guidance is given as to how to tailor agile working to allow individuals to more effectively use work-email.

Keywords Work-email · Resources · Goals · Personality ·
Agile working · Well-being

E. Russell (✉)
University of Sussex Business School (USBS), University of Sussex,
Brighton, UK
e-mail: emma.russell@sussex.ac.uk

C. Grant and E. Russell (eds.), *Agile Working and Well-Being
in the Digital Age*, https://doi.org/10.1007/978-3-030-60283-3_4

4.1   INTRODUCTION

Agile working practices increasingly involve connecting with new technologies in order to operate more flexibly, efficiently and responsively. Electronic mail (or email) is one technology that particularly enables this, owing to its anywhere, anytime, anyplace functionality. Since email was widely introduced to working life in the mid-1990s, it has clearly evolved in conjunction with worker needs to be more agile, freeing people from traditional time and space work boundaries, allowing accessibility to multiple clients and colleagues, and enabling the management of multiple projects and task strands [30].

Email was originally conceived purely as a work-messaging tool and was usually accessed by dialling up (maybe once or twice a day) to a remote server to retrieve new mail [34]. In the years that followed, and with the introduction of broadband, Wi-Fi and 4G/5G technology, email has developed to a point where as long as one's device (PC, tablet, laptop or smartphone) is enabled, then workers can connect to their work at any time. Further, the email system has become multi-purpose, a place where people store and organise work projects, calendar information, contact details, communication histories and shared documents [30]. It is perhaps unsurprising to note that globally over 281 billion email messages were sent per day in 2018, and that 86% of professionals name email as being their favoured computer-mediated communication (CMC) tool [24]. Although there are many other new contenders vying for position as the CMC tool of choice (especially social networking tools such as Slack, Yammer, mobile working volatile resources, Jabber, MS Teams, etc.) email continues to dominate because of its prevalence with workers across industries and nations [9].

In this chapter, the extent to which email, as a key work tool, allows people to engage in effective agile working practices will be discussed. In reviewing email's effectiveness, we pay particular attention to well-being as a key outcome of concern to scholars in management and psychology [23, 27] (see Chapter 1 for a definition of well-being). When well-being is considered alongside performance and goal achievement outcomes, work-email activity is often found to have a contradictory impact on effectiveness [30]. In this chapter, these contradictory effects are explored, with a particular focus on why individual differences matter when elucidating effectiveness in email-use.

4.2 DOES WORK-EMAIL FACILITATE AGILE WORKING?

Despite its popularity and apparent suitability for enabling agile working, work-email presents something of a paradox. It appears to offer many benefits, especially in terms of the achievement of work and performance goals, e.g. allowing greater temporal and geographical flexibility in communication [21], enabling timely and convenient responsiveness to clients and colleagues [16], removing status barriers and increasing accessibility [26]. Yet, there are also a number of drawbacks. For example, people report being overloaded by email [8], which can be used as a malign monitoring tool (via cc, audit trails, and unsolicited forwarding) [20]. In the absence of non-verbal cues, email communication can be misinterpreted [21] and incivility can also blight exchanges [22]. In addition, because work-extendable technologies (WETs) allow the admittance of work-email into personal time, work-life balance may suffer [15], and strain may ensue when psychological detachment from work is prevented [5]. These negative outcomes are focused around the impact on both the work performance and well-being of workers. This demonstrates the importance of research that considers both well-being and work performance as inherent to our understanding of effectiveness.

From a psychological perspective, understanding the mechanisms that might be responsible for such contrasting experiences is key. Over the past 25 years, research has aligned in concluding that when context, task and technology are fit for purpose, email can be used effectively (i.e. can facilitate both work performance and well-being). Work cultures and organisations that view email as a work-critical tool [31], that promote respect and trust in others when communicating [21], that train people in how to use email systems optimally, and which clarify email etiquette and expectations (e.g. via appropriate modelling by senior personnel) [6, 14], are associated with overall effective email use. When the fidelity of the email tool matches the demands of the job, and the capabilities of workers, work-email activity is also improved [7]. These situational parameters are useful to consider in understanding people's experience of email, yet they do not account for the important factor of individual differences in working preference.

4.3   The Role of Personality
in Understanding Effective Work-Email Use

Emerging research suggests that in order to fully understand why dealing with work-email can positively impact some people, but negatively affect others (even when the situational parameters have parity), we need to look at individual differences, such as personality. Personality comprises the stable, trait-based characteristics that reflect the thoughts, feelings and behaviours of individuals and typify how they respond across situations and time [2, 30]. People have different preferences about how they work and different people are focused on different goals [3]. If people are working towards (or achieving) a goal that they personally value, they will experience heightened well-being [3]. However, if workers act out of accordance with their natural goals and values, this can have a negative impact [32].

To understand how personality relates to effective work-email activity in agile working, there are three different research strands worth considering. First is the literature on boundary management preferences [18, 19], which has uncovered individual differences in terms of how people prefer to transition between work and life domains. Second, trait activation theory (TAT [32, 33]) and the theory of purposeful work behaviour (TPWB [3, 4]) discuss how situational cues (such as work-email) can trigger certain trait-goal activities. Third, the literature relating to personal resources and goals, specifically the Conservation of Resources (COR) model [12], examines the individual pursuit and protection of resources in relation to personally valued goals [12]. Each of these research strands is examined in relation to work-email and well-being in the following sections.

4.3.1   Preferences for Managing Work-Home Boundaries

Over the last twenty years or so, there has been a steady increase in the number of workers who are undertaking their normal work duties but flexing between when and where they operate, via the use of WETs, such as smartphones [9, 15]. The extent to which we allow or enjoy the blurring of boundaries between work and home life depends in part on our boundary management preferences (see Chapter 3). Operating on a continuum [1], it appears that people tend towards a preference either for separating home and life domains (segmenters), or—at the other end of the scale—allowing work and home to be fully integrated (integrators) [18]. At each extreme, segmenters prefer not to deal with or share personal/home issues when they are engaged with work; integrators however will be happy to blend both aspects of their lives and are likely to easily transition between domains.

The research literature has long suggested that segmenters will experience depleted well-being when engaging in work out-of-hours [19]. In a recent study [28], 35 workers reported on the amount of out-of-hours digital work they engaged in across 4 working days. In addition, workers completed a well-being diary at the end of each working day. It was confirmed that those with higher segmentation preference experienced worsened well-being in line with the amount of out-of-hours connectivity they engaged in. Interestingly, this research [28] also found that those with higher preferences for integration reported fluctuations in well-being according to the amount of out-of-hours work they had engaged in—namely the *more* they were connected to work, the higher their well-being. Although a small study, this is fascinating in demonstrating that integrators actively enjoy being connected to work outside of hours. Future research into this area could now explore whether there is an optimum level of out-of-hours connectivity for integrators, before their well-being plateaus or depletes, and whether these positive outcomes persist over the longer term. Either way, the learning from this study is that people need to be able to exercise their preferences for out-of-hours digital working, if they are to maximise their well-being in agile working contexts.

4.3.2   Trait-Relevant Goal Pursuit and Agile Working

The premise of TAT is that situational cues activate or suppress people's personality traits at work [32, 33]. When activated, people engage in behaviours that are trait-relevant and rewarding. When traits are suppressed, people may experience depleted well-being, specifically in relation to strain or dissatisfaction [32]. Relatedly, the TPWB suggests that at work, people are striving towards any of four goals, related to achievement (e.g. doing well at work), communion (e.g. engaging with other people), status (e.g. attaining positions of power or control) and autonomy (e.g. having control over work) [3]. People engage in actions that support these goals. Personality traits from the five-factor model

(FFM)[1] [2] predict which goals have the most salience for different people. For example, in terms of the TPWB, conscientious people are said to be most interested in achievement goals, agreeable people are most interested in communion goals. Acting in accordance with goals will result in people experiencing heightened well-being (via a sense of meaning and purpose) [4].

Several studies have looked at how traits and goals interact, in the context of people's work-email activity. For example, in one study [29] participants were asked to report how they had dealt with every email that had interrupted them across the course of a working day. Conscientious people were found to be more likely to be able to resist new email interruptions and stay focused on their current work task. This was predictable as conscientious people prioritise achievement goals. However, when asked, conscientious people did not report that this strategy had helped them to achieve their work goals, and they also reported that their well-being was depleted (potentially because they knew work was waiting for them via email, and they were having to resist it). As a result of this study, it was suggested that conscientious people could avoid detrimental effects if they switched their email notifications off, thus reducing their awareness of email interruptions. Future research is now needed to understand if such actions provide conscientious people with more appropriate and trait-relevant cues, and whether well-being and goal achievement improve as a result.

In another recent paper, [30] participants were asked about the actions they use to deal with work email, and the goals towards which these are focused. For example, writing short and clear work email might have been helpful both in achieving work goals, and in showing concern for colleagues. However, switching off email notifications out-of-hours could support well-being goals, but have a negative impact on a worker's desire to stay in control of their work. A large-scale survey ($N = 341$) showed that the goals that people prioritise in dealing with work-email can be predicted by personality traits [30].

---

[1] FFM traits refer to Conscientiousness (hard-working and organised), Neuroticism (anxious and worrying), Extraversion (sociable and outgoing), Openness (curious and open-minded) and Agreeableness (affable and obliging).

4.3.3   *Resources and Effective Agile Working*

The COR model indicates that people strive to conserve, protect and acquire resources, during work activity, in order to achieve valued goals. Resources may be volatile (easily expended) or key (utilised to help pursue other resources but are rarely depleted) [12]. The resources that relate to well-being (e.g. energy, happiness) may be considered to be volatile, whilst personality characteristics could be considered key resources, but only if they facilitate resource acquisition or prevent resource loss [12, 17]. In examining work-email research, the boundary management study reported above [28] shows that when people need to deal with customers out-of-hours, having a personal preference for boundary integration is clearly a useful key resource that helps a worker to build other resources (well-being) [28]. However, in a role that involves dealing with frequent email interruptions, Conscientiousness is unlikely to act as a key resource, as it fails to prevent resource loss (reduced well-being) or facilitate resource gain (work-goal achievement) [29]. Other studies have shown that traits associated with Neuroticism predict more strain and overload, and lower levels of effectiveness, when dealing with work-email [11, 13, 25]. More research is clearly needed in this area, to better understand when and whether personality acts as a key resource in agile working.

It is clear that to achieve effective outcomes (attaining work performance and heightened well-being) individuals need to be able to deal with work-email in a way that suits their personal preferences and helps them to achieve the goals that are important to them [29]. This does not mean that it is not important for organisations and systems designers to think about how they should also configure appropriate work parameters through improved job/system design and support. When the context, task and technology work optimally, there is less pressure on resources, and people will generally cope better [7]. However, the research reported above suggests that beyond these factors, we need to consider individual preferences and personality, to fully appreciate how best to build resources when engaging with work-email.

4.4   LIMITATIONS AND IMPLICATIONS FOR FUTURE RESEARCH IN THIS FIELD

Well-being is considered to be as important as performance/goal achievement outcomes in understanding if work-email activity is effective. Yet, a focus on the durability or accumulation of well-being effects, particularly over long periods, is largely missing from the extant literature. For example, whilst the four-day diary study [28] looked at well-being effects over a short period, it would be interesting to understand how well-being is impacted over more prolonged periods (a week, a fortnight, a month or more). TAT suggests that when traits are repeatedly suppressed, this can have a significant long-term impact on well-being [32, 33]. Equally, when a situation becomes stronger than the trait [1, 17] (e.g. if too much pressure is put on integrators to deal with work outside of hours to the point where they have little opportunity to engage in daily recovery), it is likely that their natural preferences for blurring boundaries will no longer alleviate the potentially stress-inducing impact of the circumstances on their well-being [10]. These issues need further exploration in future longitudinal research.

In line with this, if well-being is depleted, it may impact the extent to which people respond favourably to agile working environments. In most research within this domain, actions in relation to work-email are seen as predictors of well-being outcomes [30]. Yet, it would be interesting to examine the life cycle of action-outcome-action-outcome relationships in more detail; if well-being is depleted then people may consequently withdraw from work-email use, out-of-hours connectivity, etc. For example, following the study on Conscientiousness [29], it was suggested that conscientious people should turn off email notifications to improve their well-being when engaged in digital work. Whether such resource protecting strategies then serve to rebuild resources [12], and the extent to which personality moderates or mediate this, will be of interest in future research.

4.5   IMPLICATIONS FOR PRACTICE AND THEORY

By utilising theories of boundary management, trait-activation, and resources to explore how agile working practices relate to work-email use, we can better understand paradoxes of work-email: why dealing with work-email will sometimes create negative effects for workers and will sometimes create positive effects for workers. Research has shown that work-email may have positive impacts when resources are abundant (especially when personality acts as a key resource), and valued goals are being met. However, when resources are depleted, traits suppressed or goals unattained, dealing with work email can have negative consequences for people. It is now recommended that individual differences be considered when exploring a range of other agile working practices and in relation to other digital technologies. For example, does personality influence who is more likely to be attracted to, and work well in agile co-working hubs (as described in Chapter 12)? Are certain people better able to facilitate effective working in cross-cultural work teams (see Chapter 10)? Do individual differences impact who is better able to cope with constant digital distractions from different sources (see Chapter 5)? Exploring such pathways should elucidate the applicability of trait, resource and boundary theories for understanding agile working.

Although research into this field continues to shed new light on effectiveness in agile working practices, there are, nevertheless, a number of evidence-based recommendations relating to work-email activity that organisations and workers can begin to put in place. To facilitate effective outcomes, in terms of both well-being and work performance concerns, the following suggestions are made:

(a) It is recommended that organisations avoid putting in place blanket policies relating to how work-email should be used (e.g. email-free Fridays, banning out-of-hours work). People have different personal preferences about their work-email use and need to be given flexibility about how best to achieve their goals and support their well-being.

(b) By considering how different people (personalities) might prefer to work with email, managers can adapt strategies to appropriately meet workers' needs. For example, conscientious people might prefer to turn off notifications, so that they do not feel pressure that they are missing something and to manage interruptions effectively.

(c) In roles where people need to be available at varying times of the day and night (e.g. in global work), integrators may especially perform well, and enjoy this (with the caveat that longer-term research into resource loss and the impact on well-being is needed). Thus, integration preference could be examined at selection stages for jobs with highly blurred boundaries.

(d) Segmenters, on the other hand, may work better in environments that specify and respect clear temporal, physical and psychological boundaries between work and home life. Managers need to be mindful of these preferences, and workers would also benefit from understanding whether the demands of the job role are likely to suit their natural tendencies, communicating expectations and preferences where possible.

4.6   Conclusions

The findings outlined in this chapter indicate how the paradoxes of work-email can be explained by considering people's individual personality characteristics, as evidenced in fields relating to boundary preferences, trait-goal activity and resource theory. When people can act in accordance with their predilection towards certain goals and personal preferences, and when they have the resources to do so, they are more likely to experience heightened well-being, without this being at the expense of work performance. This is considered to be effective work-email activity. It will be interesting to examine whether personality differences impact people's use of other emerging and increasingly popular CMC tools now, to further elucidate how personality preference impacts activity that facilitates both performance and well-being. In essence, research into the role of personality in agile working practices cannot be ignored if we want to advise people about effective CMC use both now and in the future. Allowing people to tailor their approach appears to be the optimal way forward.

References

1. Ashforth, B. E., Kreiner, G. E., & Fugate, M. (2000). All in a day's work: Boundaries and micro role transitions. *Academy of Management Review, 25*(3), 472–491. https://doi.org/10.2307/259305.
2. Barrick, M. R., & Mount, M. K. (1991). The big five personality dimensions and job performance: A meta-analysis. *Personnel Psychology, 44*(1), 1–26. https://doi.org/10.1111/j.1744-6570.1991.tb00688.x.
3. Barrick, M. R., Mount, M. K., & Li, N. (2013). The theory of purposeful work behavior: The role of personality, higher-order goals, and job characteristics. *Academy of Management Review, 38*(1), 132–153. https://psycnet.apa.org/doi/10.5465/amr.2010.0479.
4. Barrick, M. R., Stewart, G. L., & Piotrowski, M. (2002). Personality and job performance: Test of the mediating effects of motivation among sales representatives. *Journal of Applied Psychology, 87*(1), 43–51. https://doi.org/10.1037/0021-9010.87.1.43.
5. Braukmann, J., Schmitt, A., Ďuranová, L., & Ohly, S. (2018). Identifying ICT-related affective events across life domains and examining their unique relationships with employee recovery. *Journal of Business and Psychology, 33*(4), 529–544. https://doi.org/10.1007/s10869-017-9508-7.
6. Burgess, A., Jackson, T., & Edwards, J. (2005). Email training significantly reduces email defects. *International Journal of Information Management, 25*(1), 71–83. https://doi.org/10.1016/j.ijinfomgt.2004.10.004.

7. Burton-Jones, A., & Grange, C. (2013). From use to effective use: A representation theory perspective. *Information Systems Research, 24*(3), 632–658. https://doi.org/10.1287/isre.1120.0444.

8. Dabbish, L. A., & Kraut, R. E. (2006). Email overload at work: An analysis of factors associated with email strain. *Proceedings of the 2006 20th Anniversary Conference on Computer Supported Cooperative Work, New York,* ACM, 431–440. https://doi.org/10.1145/1180875.1180941.

9. Ellis, D. A. (2019). Are smartphones really that bad? Improving the psychological measurement of technology-related behaviors. *Computers in Human Behavior, 97,* 60–66. https://doi.org/10.1016/j.chb.2019.03.006.

10. Gadeyne, N., Verbruggen, M., Delanoeije, J., & De Cooman, R. (2018). All wired, all tired? Work-related ICT-use outside work hours and work-to-home conflict: The role of integration preference, integration norms and work demands. *Journal of Vocational Behavior, 107,* 86–99. https://doi.org/10.1016/j.jvb.2018.03.008.

11. Hair, M., Renaud, K. V., & Ramsay, J. (2007). The influence of self-esteem and locus of control on perceived email-related stress. *Computers in Human Behavior, 23*(6), 2791–2803. https://doi.org/10.1016/j.chb.2006.05.005.

12. Hobfoll, S. E., Halbesleben, J., Neveu, J. P., & Westman, M. (2018). Conservation of resources in the organizational context: The reality of resources and their consequences. *Annual Review of Organizational Psychology and Organizational Behavior, 5,* 103–128. https://doi.org/10.1146/annurev-orgpsych-032117-104640.

13. Huang, E. Y., & Lin, S. W. (2014). How does email use affect perceived control of time? *Information & Management, 51*(6), 679–687. https://doi.org/10.1016/j.im.2014.05.013.

14. Huang, E. Y., Lin, S. W., & Lin, S. C. (2011). A quasi-experiment approach to study the effect of email management training. *Computers in Human Behavior, 27*(1), 522–531. https://doi.org/10.1016/j.chb.2010.09.021.

15. Hunter, E. M., Clark, M. A., & Carlson, D. S. (2019). Violating work-family boundaries: Reactions to interruptions at work and home. *Journal of Management, 45*(3), 1284–1308. https://doi.org/10.1177/0149206317702221.

16. Im, H. G. (2006). *In sync over distance: Flexible coordination through communication in geographically distributed software development work.* Unpublished doctoral thesis. Massachusetts Institute of Technology. http://hdl.handle.net/1721.1/40393.

17. Judge, T. A., & Zapata, C. P. (2015). The person–situation debate revisited: Effect of situation strength and trait activation on the validity of the Big Five personality traits in predicting job performance. *Academy of Management Journal, 58*(4), 1149–1179. https://doi.org/10.5465/amj.2010.0837.

18. Kossek, E. E., Lautsch, B. A., & Eaton, S. C. (2006). Telecommuting, control, and boundary management: Correlates of policy use and practice, job control, and work–family effectiveness. *Journal of Vocational Behavior, 68*(2), 347–367. https://doi.org/10.1016/j.jvb.2005.07.002.

19. Kreiner, G. E. (2006). Consequences of work-home segmentation or integration: A person-environment fit perspective. *Journal of Organizational Behavior, 27*(4), 485–507. https://doi.org/10.1002/job.386.

20. Lee, J. Y. H., Panteli, N., Bülow, A. M., & Hsu, C. (2018). Email adaptation for conflict handling: A case study of cross-border inter organisational partnership in East Asia. *Information Systems Journal, 28*(2), 318–339. https://doi.org/10.1111/isj.12139.

21. Nurmi, N. (2011). Coping with coping strategies: how distributed teams and their members deal with the stress of distance, time zones and culture. *Stress and Health, 27*(2), 123–143. https://doi.org/10.1002/smi.1327.

22. Park, Y., Fritz, C., & Jex, S. M. (2018). Daily cyber incivility and distress: The moderating roles of resources at work and home. *Journal of Management, 44*(7), 2535–2557. https://doi.org/10.1177/0149206315576796.

23. Quick, J. C., Macik-Frey, M., & Cooper, C. L. (2007). Managerial dimensions of organizational health: The healthy leader at work. *Journal of Management Studies, 44*(2), 189–205. https://doi.org/10.1111/j.1467-6486.2007.00684.x.

24. Radicati Group. (2018). *Email Statistics Report 2018–2022.* https://www.radicati.com/wp/wp-content/uploads/2018/01/Email_Statistics_Report,_2018-2022_Executive_Summary.pdf. Accessed 22 January 2020.

25. Reinke, K., & Chamorro-Premuzic, T. (2014). When email use gets out of control: Understanding the relationship between personality and email overload and the impact on burnout and work engagement. *Computers in Human Behavior, 36*, 502–509. https://doi.org/10.1016/j.chb.2014.03.075.

26. Rosen, C. C., Simon, L. S., Gajendran, R. S., Johnson, R. E., Lee, H. W., & Lin, S. H. J. (2019). Boxed in by your inbox: Implications of daily email demands for managers' leadership behaviors. *Journal of Applied Psychology, 104*(1), 19–33. https://psycnet.apa.org/doi/10.1037/apl0000343.

27. Russell, E., & Daniels, K. (2018). Measuring affective well-being at work using short-form scales: Implications for affective structures and participant instructions. *Human Relations, 71*(11), 1478–1507. https://doi.org/10.1177/0018726717751034.

28. Russell, E., Laing, K. & Grant, C. A. (2019, May 29–June 1). *Always On? Or are we? An investigation into the moderating effect of boundary management strategies on the relationship between after-hours work and well-being.*

Conference presentation. 19th Congress of the European Association of Work and Organizational Psychology (EAWOP), Turin, Italy.

29. Russell, E., Woods, S. A., & Banks, A. P. (2017). Examining conscientiousness as a key resource in resisting email interruptions: implications for volatile resources and goal achievement. *Journal of Occupational and Organizational Psychology, 90*(3), 407–435. https://psycnet.apa.org/doi/10.1111/joop.12177.

30. Russell, E., & Woods, S. A. (2020). Personality differences as predictors of action-goal relationships in work-email activity. *Computers in Human Behavior, 103,* 67–79. https://doi.org/10.1016/j.chb.2019.09.022.

31. Sumecki, D., Chipulu, M., & Ojiako, U. (2011). Email overload: Exploring the moderating role of the perception of email as a 'business critical' tool. *Journal of Information Management, 31*(5), 407–414. https://doi.org/10.1016/j.ijinfomgt.2010.12.008.

32. Tett, R. P., & Burnett, D. D. (2003). A personality trait-based interactionist model of job performance. *Journal of Applied Psychology, 88*(3), 500–517. https://psycnet.apa.org/doi/10.1037/0021-9010.88.3.500.

33. Tett, R. P., Simonet, D. V., Walser, B., & Brown, C. (2013). Trait activation theory. In N. Christiansen & R. Tett (Eds.), *Handbook of personality at work* (pp. 71–100). Hove: Routledge.

34. Whittaker, S., & Sidner, C. (1996). Email overload: exploring personal information management of email. *Proceedings of the SIGCHI conference on Human factors in computing systems, Vancouver, Canada* 276–283. https://doi.org/10.1145/238386.238530.

CHAPTER 5

Digital Distractions: The Effect and Use of Digital Message Alerts and Their Relationship with Work-Life Balance

Maria Uther, Michelle Cleveland, and Rhiannon Jones

Abstract Agile working in contemporary society necessarily involves using technology to work flexibly across different locations, time zones, etc. To be able to respond to an agile working environment, employees often keep digital notifications switched on, yet we know little about the potential impact this has on employee well-being and ability to function effectively at work. This chapter will focus on the role of physiological responses (as an index of hypervigilance) to digital messaging alerts and whether indices of heightened vigilance are associated with perceptions

M. Uther (✉)
University of Wolverhampton, Wolverhampton, UK
e-mail: M.Uther@wlv.ac.uk

M. Cleveland · R. Jones
University of Winchester, Winchester, UK
e-mail: Michelle.Cleveland@winchester.ac.uk

R. Jones
e-mail: Rhiannon.Jones@winchester.ac.uk

of poor work-life balance. We demonstrate that messaging alerts show evidence of heightened attentional switches in the brain, whilst neural measures of individual's perceived balance between their work and non-work roles suggest a potentially vicious cycle of fatigue and hypervigilance accompanying poor work-life balance. Within this chapter, we explore these findings and consider how to reduce the cycle of physiological hypervigilance from poor work-life balance.

Keywords Distractions · Notifications · Alerts · Digital · Email · Work-life balance · Vigilance

5.1   Introduction

In the modern world of work, we are continually interrupted by a barrage of digital notifications (from email, text messages, instant messenger systems, social media, etc.) attempting to grab our attention and get us to move away from our task and towards the senders'. This chapter seeks to understand how the characteristics of digital notifications command workers' attention and impact employee well-being and their perception of balance between work and non-work roles. In particular, we review evidence around the use of auditory alerts. For example, loud and repetitive alerts may seize attention but create stress. Softer, short-duration alerts may not create a stress response but may fail to be noticed, potentially allowing the end-user to miss critical messages. To this end, we suggest evidence-based best practices that reduce the amount of needless arousal demands, without compromising the notification of critical messages. By applying this knowledge to the use of people's work communication tools, we suggest how to reduce the negative impact of digital communications on people's well-being and work-life balance, without causing work performance to suffer. In this chapter, we also provide a starting point for software designers of messaging alerts to deliver notifications in a manner that reduces stress but does not compromise attention to urgent messages.

In agile working environments, we are especially reliant on 'work extendable technologies' (WETs) e.g. laptops and mobile phones. Virtually all of these technologies emit audible alerts: often coupled with a visual mode unless the user elects to turn these off. Intuitively, we know how intrusive auditory alerts are; many people switch mobile phones off for meetings, at the cinema or at a child's school performance. Yet within our day-to-day use of these technologies at work, audible notifications are often kept on, leaving workers open to distraction. At a purely physical level, there is considerable research evidence guiding the sensible use of sounds as alerts, with some types of digital alerts suggested to be more distracting/intrusive/stress-inducing than others, as a result of their physical properties (see [18, 21] for a review). For example, extremely loud sounds (above 85–100 dB[1]) will induce startle responses that will disrupt workflow negatively and indeed can impede overall performance [9, 23]. Similarly, high-pitched sounds will be more arousing than low-pitched sounds and higher amplitude sounds are more arousing compared to low amplitude sounds, such that they are perceived as more urgent [11, 13]. Seminal work by Patterson and colleagues has also provided useful guidelines on the use of auditory warnings [21] in terms of recommendations for maximum number of simultaneous warnings as well as overall physical qualities. Similar guidelines have been developed for safety-critical environments [e.g., 2, 12]. For example, there is an abundance of research on the immediate effects of mobile phone use within safety-critical contexts such as driving [17, 35, 37] and healthcare settings [10]. However, there is little research evidence for the use of auditory alerts in non-safety critical environments.

In particular, the immediate (as opposed to long-term) nature of disruption of non-safety-critical alerts has not been systematically studied within office-based work contexts, or indeed outside of contracted or usual working hours. There is therefore a clear gap in the research on the immediate impact of digital messaging alerts on well-being (e.g. hypervigilance effects) and work-life balance within non-safety-critical contexts (e.g. ordinary office-based environments). From a design point of view, the urgency of notifications has to be balanced against annoyance of stress. In the case of an 'annoying' sound, it may simply be ignored; in the case of an extremely startling sound, it can impair performance. Determining the balance between the ability to notify vs. annoy/create stress is important, although urgency and annoyance may not always be correlated [16, 19]. Despite the fact that auditory warnings could be voluntarily ignored, evidence suggests that there is an attentional cost to primary performance if the alert is unattended. For example, mobile phone notifications cause interference on an attentionally-demanding task even when ignored [34].

---

[1] Decibels.

It is also clear that apart from physical factors, individual differences and psychological factors are at play in the degree to which auditory alerts are perceived as intrusive. For example, researchers [23] note that there are considerable individual differences related to susceptibility to disruption by different physical properties of auditory signals. Whether these individual differences are related to individual traits (e.g. Neuroticism) remains to be empirically tested. Another relevant psychological aspect is the controllability of an alert [32]. Any alert or notification that 'interrupts' an existing work task, has the potential to be disruptive because it diverts attention from the interrupted task, thereby requiring cognitive resources to hold either the unfinished work task or interruption in working memory, or involving recovery processes to adjust to task-switching [37, 40]. However, if the interruption can be controlled by the recipient, these disruptive effects can be somewhat mitigated [22, 24]. When people have control over their work, they select the most optimal course of action to ensure efficiency [8]. This is a key tenet of most contemporary theories of stress. When control over one's work is low, strain is higher [15]. The relevance of 'controllability' is critical to the implementation of current digital alerts. Current systems generally default to a 'push' style of notification (i.e. the system notifies the user) rather than a 'pull' style, whereby the end-user executes their own agency to check the system for notifications; a 'pull' system may actually be more optimal for the user.

5.2   KEY FINDINGS FROM RESEARCH IN THE FIELD OF DIGITAL DISTRACTIONS

What is clear from research in this field is that it may not necessarily be the physical properties (so much as the meaning of the sound) that grab the user's attention and leads to potential overload. In an initial study [38], email alerts (in particular, the Microsoft Outlook sound) were processed differently by the brain compared to the mobile message alerts (specifically the 'Android whistle' sound). The email alert sound generated a greater positive activity of around 400 ms post-stimulus in scalp frontal regions compared to matched distractors, despite smaller physical differences between the target sounds and distractors, see Fig. 5.1. This pattern of activity would likely be an indicator of attentional 'switch' to novel or significant sounds [20, 32].

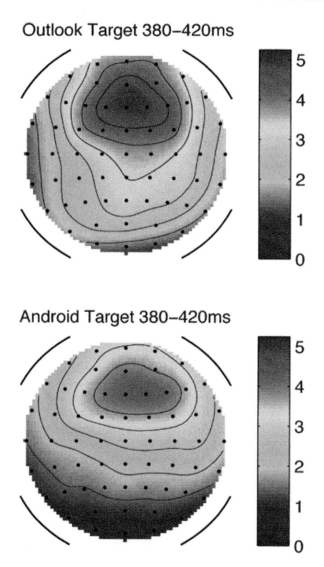

Fig. 5.1   Late positive responses to two different kinds of digital distractors (Outlook email and Android mobile phone message). Adapted from Uther et al. [38]

Faster reaction times to Outlook sounds were also correlated with higher job involvement, but not for Android sounds. These data suggest that 'work-related' sounds may be given more attentional 'weight' compared to other sounds. In a further study [14], the neural corre-lates of perceived work-life balance were investigated using both trait and state electroencephalogram (EEG) alpha measures. Neural activity in the alpha band reflects the proportion of neuronal populations firing at a rate of 8–12 Hz.[2] Variations in the magnitude, or power of activity in this frequency band when an individual is resting reflect differences in enduring qualities, such as personality or baseline levels of arousal; in contrast, patterns of alpha activity occurring during the performance of a task reflect individual differences in the processing of a stimulus—partic-ularly regarding the ability to inhibit irrelevant or distracting information. It was predicted that dissatisfaction with the balance between work and non-work roles would be associated with increased resting alpha power, consistent with studies of burnout, and diminished alpha response to distractor sounds, thereby indicating difficulty in suppressing automatic responses to work-related stimuli [14]. Significant correlations between self-reported measures of work/non-work balance and both resting, and task-related alpha responses, supported these predictions. Together these data suggest that dissatisfaction with work/non-work balance is associated with state hypervigilance to work-related cues, and a trait neural marker of fatigue, both symptomatic of lowered cognitive capacity [14]. Overall, the results from these two studies are also in line with other data showing that meaningful or 'personally significant' sounds elicit P3a-type (attentional switch) responses that are different in morphology/timing to 'regular' attentional changes [e.g. 28, 33, 38, 39].

Existing work-life balance literature can offer relevant theoretical foun-dations to build an understanding as to how immediate physiological responses to digital message alerts can feed into longer-term stress. Firstly, border and boundary theories [1, 5] offer an insight into the longer-term effects of digital message alerts within the context of work and non-work. For example, such theories would suggest that the crossing of one domain into the other can have negative consequences on the management of work and non-work life (see Chapter 3), whilst minimising communi-cation strain and effectively managing the boundaries between work and

[2] I.e. indicative of brain activity or arousal.

non-work life can reduce stress [25, 26]. Such findings, therefore, provide an understanding of how disruption from message alerts has the potential to negatively impact employees in the long term. The key findings from the authors' research extend this knowledge by providing some initial understanding of the immediate impact that disruption from such message alerts can have.

Secondly, balance, which is distinct from perceiving conflict and/or enrichment of the roles and responsibilities in work/non-work [3], can be considered multidimensional in nature. It has been identified that satisfaction, effectiveness, involvement and fit are fundamental components that provide a basis for perceived balance, or imbalance, between work and non-working roles and responsibilities [4]. Effectively managing the roles in work and non-work life is important in the sense of contentment or satisfaction with the balance between these roles, something that existing literature has identified. A perceived lack of balance between work and non-work life can lead to feelings of job strain [7], whilst a dissatisfaction with perceived balance can negatively impact on psychological well-being and contribute to occupational burnout [6, 27]. Balance, or a perception of balance, can therefore contribute to the well-being of employees and, as suggested by the authors' follow-up study, a sense of dissatisfaction with such balance contributes to an attentional bias towards digital message alerts of a work-related nature. The consequences of which, may be a vicious cycle of poor work-life balance and continued work-related biases in attention.

5.3   Limitations in the Field and Implications for Future Research

In terms of future research, there is clearly much more to be done. We know that digital message alerts produce patterns of brain activity that index specific attentional switches. However, it also appears that the exact pattern of attentional switch for meaningful sounds may differ compared to that of attentional switches caused by, for example, particularly loud sounds. In our study, we found that the Outlook (work-related) sounds elicited larger responses, demonstrating attention 'switch' in the brain compared to ordinary (non-work related) messaging sounds. The observed pattern of responses differed from usual patterns of attention-switch to particularly loud sounds (i.e. the signal was larger in the frontal regions as opposed to the frequently observed pattern of larger activity in the central or parietal regions). Other studies [e.g. 36, 39] also showed that there were similar (frontally maximal) responses in response to other meaningful sounds.

Although we see a different scalp distribution of activity to attention switch in other contexts, it still remains to be seen whether this demonstrates different neural processing/origin. Only further studies using, for example, source localisation methods could ascertain this. The other area requiring further research is in the field of individual differences. We know, for example, that in the relatively small sample (around 30), there may be individual differences at a neural level in terms of heightened physiological arousal; this appears to drive other individual differences in coping and resilience [30, 32]. Yet, it is clear that more research is needed to understand physiological reactivity to work-related messages, to understand how digital distractions affect, and are affected by long term, stable factors, such as personality.

Another consideration is that the body of evidence presented here only addresses the use of auditory digital distractions. Clearly, these are very attention-grabbing, which is why we often intuitively switch our devices to silent. Yet, further work is needed to determine whether visual-only alerts are less distracting in terms of work productivity than auditory ones. Future work could, for example, examine whether the physiological arousal from the use of auditory alerts vs visual-only alerts is equivalent. As the use of digital technologies is so prevalent in today's agile working environment, we need more urgent work to understand interruptibility factors in this field.

5.4   PRACTICAL AND THEORETICAL IMPLICATIONS OF RESEARCH FINDINGS

The research outlined within this chapter offers two important contributions to the literature. Firstly, that when a message alert is meaningful, in this case a work-related message alert, coupled with problematic job involvement, there is a heightened sensitivity to the alert (the alert is attended to more quickly). Secondly, that dissatisfaction with perceived balance between work and non-work contributes to an unconscious attentional-bias towards work-related stimuli. Whilst the exploratory nature of this research must be considered, taken together, these findings would suggest that poor work-life balance is linked to a sense of attentional bias and hypervigilance towards work-related message alerts that has the potential to contribute negatively to employee well-being.

The social pressure that is invariably coupled with work-related email cannot be ignored here, particularly in relation to the attentional bias shown towards these email alerts. Work-related emails are, for the most part, related to distributing and carrying out tasks, which inevitably carries a level of social pressure. Email received outside of working hours, and the decision taken to open the email or not, also comes with a level of social pressure, or expectation [29, 31]. The constant bombardment of work-related email to our devices could be leading to an attentional bias via a conditioned emotional response to these alerts. The very early stage that processing this information occurs at suggests that people are perceiving these alerts as negative, in the sense that they are hypervigilant to a potential threat. It is likely that these alerts can be intrusive to the worker's 'flow' and that in turn is contributing to the fatigue being experienced by those who perceive poor balance between their work and non-work lives.

The research outlined in this chapter contributes to understanding as to why some employees find it difficult to manage demands on their time when engaging in agile working. Frequent attentional switching, when hearing the familiar 'work-email' alert, and the attentional bias associated with receiving work-related message alerts, are linked with perceptions of poor balance between work-life and home-life. As such, this relationship can contribute to a vicious cycle of feeling fatigue whilst remaining hypervigilant to the potential for further incoming alerts.

There are some easily actioned recommendations that can be made based on this research, for both individual employees and managers/organisations. Individual employees may wish to change the way in which they receive messages from their devices; moving from a 'push' mode to a 'pull' mode, so they are more active and in control in the retrieval of work-related messages. Alternatively, some employees may prefer to remove the alert tones from their devices altogether, particularly when they are not in work. These simple acts could help to minimise the frequent attention paid to incoming messages and alerts, offering some vital physiological restoration and the opportunity to engage more fully with activities in their non-working life. Organisations and employees can together address the expectation placed on staff to feel they should be, or need to be, responding to email outside of work time. One simple approach would be to set a cut-off time for sending email to colleagues in the evening, or early morning; with no email coming in, there are no message alerts that require attention. Whilst it is appreciated that this can be limiting for some, delayed email sending and draft functions can be used to manage workloads, without impacting on the well-being of colleagues. This latter action does require buy-in from all parties involved and would need to be adhered to if it were to positively contribute employee work-life balance.

The restoration of the model of the worker as choosing control over their workflow will undoubtedly be a far healthier model for the individual and is something that software designers could employ. Within agile working patterns, it is crucial that workers retain a sense of agency in their workflow, so they can remain focused on their core work tasks as needed, or indeed be able to 'switch off' at times they need to be 'at home' and not working.

5.5   Conclusions

In conclusion, it is clear that the use of auditory alerts to signal work-related messages is causing an attentional switch, such that this would be feeding into a heightened state of physiological arousal over the long term. Whilst there is further work that needs to be done to determine both the underlying neural mechanisms involved, as well as the influence of individual differences, it is clear that we need to reduce the amount of push auditory notifications to workers. This affords work to be more focused/productive and the worker less overloaded with distractions. This is becoming an increasingly important issue in an agile working environment where our dependence upon technology to connect and alert us to changing demands has never been more fundamental to our work.

References

1. Ashforth, B. E., Kreiner, G. E., & Fugate, M. (2000). All in a day's work: Boundaries and micro role transitions. *Academy of Management Review, 25*(3), 472–491. https://doi.org/10.2307/259305.
2. Baldwin, C. L. (2016). *Auditory cognition and human performance: Research and applications.* Boca Raton, FL: CRC Press.
3. Carlson, D. S., Grzywacz, J. G., & Zivnuska, S. (2009). Is work–family balance more than conflict and enrichment? *Human Relations, 62*(10), 1459–1486. https://doi.org/10.1177/0018726709336500.
4. Casper, W. J., Vaziri, H., Wayne, J. H., DeHauw, S., & Greenhaus, J. (2018). The jingle-jangle of work–nonwork balance: A comprehensive and

meta-analytic review of its meaning and measurement. *Journal of Applied Psychology, 103*(2), 182–214. https://doi.org/10.1037/apl0000259182.

5. Clark, S. C. (2000). Work/family border theory: A new theory of work/family balance. *Human Relations, 53*(6), 747–770. https://doi.org/10.1177/0018726700536001.

6. Derks, D., & Bakker, A. B. (2014). Smartphone use, work–home interference, and burnout: A diary study on the role of recovery. *Applied Psychology, 63*(3), 411–440. https://doi.org/10.1111/j.1464-0597.2012.00530.x.

7. Fisher-McAuley, G., Stanton, J., Jolton, J., & Gavin, J. (2003, April 12). *Modelling the relationship between work life balance and organisational outcomes* [Conference presentation]. Annual Conference of the Society for Industrial-Organisational Psychology, Orlando.

8. Frese, M., & Zapf, D. (1994). Action as the core of work psychology: A German approach. In H. C. Triandis, M. D. Dunnette, & L. M. Hough (Eds.), *Handbook of industrial and organizational psychology* (pp. 271–340). Palo Alto, CA: Consulting Psychologists Press.

9. Gerdes, A. B., Wieser, M. J., & Alpers, G. W. (2014). Emotional pictures and sounds: A review of multimodal interactions of emotion cues in multiple domains. *Frontiers in Psychology, 5,* 1351. https://doi.org/10.3389/fpsyg.2014.01351.

10. Gill, P. S., Kamath, A., & Gill, T. S. (2012). Distraction: An assessment of smartphone usage in health care work settings. *Risk Management and Healthcare Policy, 5,* 105–114. https://doi.org/10.2147/RMHP.S34813.

11. Hellier, E., & Edworthy, J. (1999). On using psychophysical techniques to achieve urgency mapping in auditory warnings. *Applied Ergonomics, 30*(2), 167–171. https://doi.org/10.1016/S0003-6870(97)00013-6.

12. Hellier, E., & Edworthy, J. (1999). The design and validation of attensons for a high workload environment. In J. Edworthy & N. A. Stanton (Eds.), *Human factors in auditory warnings* (pp. 283–304). New York: Routledge.

13. Hellier, E., Edworthy, J., Weedon, B., Walters, K., & Adams, A. (2002). The perceived urgency of speech warnings: Semantics versus acoustics. *Human Factors, 44*(1), 1–17. https://doi.org/10.1518/0018720024494810.

14. Jones, R., Cleveland, M., & Uther, M. (2019). State and trait neural correlates of the balance between work and nonwork roles. *Psychiatry Research: Neuroimaging, 287*(1), 19–30. https://doi.org/10.1016/j.pscychresns.2019.03.009.

15. Karasek, R., & Theorell, T. (1990). *Healthy work: Stress, productivity and the reconstruction of working life.* New York: Basic Books.

16. Lee, J. D., Hoffman, J. D., & Hayes, E. (2004). Collision warning design to mitigate driver distraction. In *Proceedings of the SIGCHI Conference on Human factors in Computing Systems, Vienna, Austria* (pp. 65–72). https://doi.org/10.1145/985692.985701.

17. Lipovac, K., Đerić, M., Tešić, M., Andrić, Z., & Marić, B. (2017). Mobile phone use while driving-literary review. *Transportation Research Part F: Traffic Psychology and Behaviour, 47*, 132–142. https://doi.org/10.1016/j.trf.2017.04.015.

18. Macken, W. J., Phelps, F. G., & Jones, D. M. (2009). What causes auditory distraction? *Psychonomic Bulletin & Review, 16*(1), 139–144. https://doi.org/10.3758/PBR.16.1.139.

19. Marshall, D. C., Lee, J. D., & Austria, P. A. (2007). Alerts for in-vehicle information systems: Annoyance, urgency, and appropriateness. *Human Factors, 49*(1), 145–157. https://doi.org/10.1518/001872007779598145.

20. Masson, R., & Bidet-Caulet, A. (2019). Fronto-central P3a to distracting sounds: An index of their arousing properties. *Neuroimage, 185*, 164–180. https://doi.org/10.1016/j.neuroimage.2018.10.041.

21. Mayfield, T., & Patterson, R. (1990). Auditory warning sounds in the work environment: Discussion. *Philosophical Transactions of the Royal Society of London Series B, Biological Sciences, 327*(1241), 485–492. http://www.jstor.org/stable/55320.

22. McFarlane, D. C. (2002). Comparison of four primary methods for coordinating the interruption of people in human-computer interaction. *Human-Computer Interaction, 17*(1), 63–139. https://doi.org/10.1207/S15327051HCI1701_2.

23. Michailidis, E., & Banks, A. P. (2016). The relationship between burnout and risk-taking in workplace decision-making and decision-making style. *Work & Stress, 30*(3), 278–292. https://doi.org/10.1080/02678373.2016.1213773.

24. Miller, S. L. (2002). Window of opportunity: Using the interruption lag to manage disruption in complex tasks. *Proceedings of the Human Factors and Ergonomics Society Annual Meeting, 46*(3), 245–249. https://doi.org/10.1177/154193120204600306.

25. Park, Y., Fritz, C., & Jex, S. M. (2011). Relationships between work-home segmentation and psychological detachment from work: The role of communication technology use at home. *Journal of Occupational Health Psychology, 16*(4), 457–467. https://doi.org/10.1037/a0023594.

26. Park, Y., & Jex, S. M. (2011). Work-home boundary management using communication and information technology. *International Journal of Stress Management, 18*(2), 133–152. https://doi.org/10.1037/a0022759.

27. Peeters, M. C., Montgomery, A. J., Bakker, A. B., & Schaufeli, W. B. (2005). Balancing work and home: How job and home demands are related to burnout. *International Journal of Stress Management, 12*(1), 43. https://doi.org/10.1037/1072-5245.12.1.43.

28. Roye, A., Jacobsen, T., & Schröger, E. (2013). Discrimination of personally significant from nonsignificant sounds: A training study. *Cognitive, Affective, & Behavioral Neuroscience, 13*(4), 930–943. https://doi.org/10.3758/s13 415-013-0173-7.

29. Russell, E. (2017). *Strategies for effectively managing email at work.* ACAS Research Report. https://archive.acas.org.uk/media/4926/Strategies-for-Effectively-Managing-Email-at-Work/pdf/Strategies-for-effectively-man aging-email-at-work.pdf. Accessed 10 August 2020.

30. Russell, E., & Woods, S. A. (2020). Personality differences as predictors of action-goal relationships in work-email activity. *Computers in Human Behavior, 103,* 67–79. https://doi.org/10.1016/j.chb.2019.09.022.

31. Russell, E., Jackson, T., & Banks, A. (2019). Classifying computer-mediated communication (CMC) interruptions at work using control as a key delineator. *(Online only). Behaviour & Information Technology,* 1–15. https://doi.org/10.1080/0144929X.2019.1683606.

32. Russell, E., Woods, S. A., & Banks, A. P. (2017). Examining conscientiousness as a key resource in resisting email interruptions: Implications for volatile resources and goal achievement. *Journal of Occupational and Organizational Psychology, 90*(3), 407–435. https://doi.org/10.1111/joop.12177.

33. SanMiguel, I., Morgan, H. M., Klein, C., Linden, D., & Escera, C. (2010). On the functional significance of novelty-P3: Facilitation by unexpected novel sounds. *Biological Psychology, 83*(2), 143–152. https://doi.org/10.1016/j.biopsycho.2009.11.012.

34. Stothart, C., Mitchum, A., & Yehnert, C. (2015). The attentional cost of receiving a cell phone notification. *Journal of Experimental Psychology: Human Perception and Performance, 41*(4), 893–897. https://doi.org/10.1037/xhp0000100.

35. Strayer, D. L., Drews, F. A., & Johnston, W. A. (2003). Cell phone-induced failures of visual attention during simulated driving. *Journal of Experimental Psychology: Applied, 9*(1), 23–32. https://doi.org/10.1037/1076-898X.9.1.23.

36. Tervaniemi, M., Janhunen, L., Kruck, S., Putkinen, V., & Huotilainen, M. (2016). Auditory profiles of classical, jazz, and rock musicians: Genre-specific sensitivity to musical sound features. *Frontiers in Psychology, 6,* 1900. https://www.frontiersin.org/article/10.3389/fpsyg.2015.01900.

37. Trafton, J. G., Altmann, E. M., Brock, D. P., & Mintz, F. E. (2003). Preparing to resume an interrupted task: Effects of prospective goal encoding and retrospective rehearsal. *International Journal of Human-Computer Studies, 58*(5), 583–603. https://doi.org/10.1016/S1071-581 9(03)00023-5.

38. Uther, M., Cleveland, M., & Jones, R. (2018). Email overload? Brain and behavioral responses to common messaging alerts are heightened for email alerts and are associated with job involvement. *Frontiers in Psychology, 9,* 1206. https://doi.org/10.3389/fpsyg.2018.01206.
39. Uther, M., Kujala, A., Huotilainen, M., Shtyrov, Y., & Näätänen, R. (2006). Training in morse code enhances involuntary attentional switching to acoustic frequency: Evidence from ERPs. *Brain Research, 1073–74,* 417–424. https://doi.org/10.1016/j.brainres.2005.12.047.
40. Wickens, C. D., Gutzwiller, R. S., & Santamaria, A. (2015). Discrete task switching in overload: A meta-analyses and a model. *International Journal of Human-Computer Studies, 79,* 79–84. https://doi.org/10.1016/j.ijhcs.2015.01.002.

CHAPTER 6

E-Resistance: Making Active Choices for Technology Management in an Agile Working Age

Deepali D'mello

Abstract The blurring of boundaries between work and non-work activity has increased in line with the advancement in New Communication Technology (NCT). Agile working, enabled by these NCTs, blurs those boundaries even further. As a consequence, workers are impelled to make active choices to resist and manage NCTs if they wish to strengthen the boundaries between work and non-work. This notion of resistance to NCTs is evidenced in the realms of social media, smartphones and generic use, but less so in the world of work-based NCTs. Lifespan Theories and Conservation of Resources theory lend a strong theoretical framework in understanding the behaviours, motivations and impact of E-Resistance— active choices of avoidance or resistance to control NCT use to balance one's resources to meet work and personal goals.

D. D'mello (✉)
University of Sussex, Brighton, UK
e-mail: d.a.dmello@sussex.ac.uk

Keywords E-Resistance · New Communication Technology ·
Conservation of Resources · Digital well-being

6.1   INTRODUCTION

Digitisation is engendering an 'always on' and 'constantly connected'
environment [24, 38]. Devices such as smartphones, laptops, smart-
watches have augmented the use of New Communication Technologies (NCT's) such as email, Slack, Skype and others. Numerous terms
are synonymous to NCT and are often documented as Information
and Communication Technology (ICT) [5], Communication and Information Technology (CIT) [28], Computer Mediated Communication
(CMC) [11] and Mobile Technologies [4]. In this chapter, NCTs are
communication technology platforms that send and receive information.
Work Extendable Technologies (WETs) are devices that enable information to be sent and received digitally, e.g. laptops, tablets, phones.
A common feature is that these technologies facilitate (and arguably
promote) agile working practices in enabling organisations and individuals
to work constantly anytime and anywhere.

Benefits of NCTs in promoting agile working are well researched.
NCTs support organisations and workers in meeting the demands of a
complex global market. Via the use of NCTs virtual team collaboration
[7], increased productivity and efficiency [6] and autonomy and flexibility
[5] allows workers to feel connected and to personalise their working
practices [4]. Nonetheless, NCT use comes with its own challenges.
Towers et al. [35] denote WETs as mobile and pervasive, facilitating
'supplemental' work at home and other locations, increasing load and
blurring boundaries between work and family life [37]. As WETs enable
extended working hours and locations this can lead to additional work
being undertaken outside their regular working hours, invading personal
time. NCT use has shown to lengthen the workday [26], increase stress
[21] and lower psychological well-being [36]. In a recent study, Mazmanian et al. [24] argued that workers experience an 'autonomy paradox',
where NCTs offer ultimate flexibility of working times and locations but
can induce psychological pressure to overwork past contracted hours.
NCTs are known to interrupt task performance and reduce thoughtful
reflection [22] potentially interrupting workers' flow and creating overload [18]. NCT-led activities and ensuing emotions can spiral from one
domain to the other [30]. Hence, NCTs that enable agile working can

also permeate and erode boundaries between work and non-work time, in a way that is problematic for well-being [20].

It is this permeability that makes boundary management a skill that can enable people to reconsider work and non-work-related priorities, including family life [39]. Porousness of boundaries, impact on productivity and reduction in overall well-being make the management of connectivity more challenging and elaborate. Individuals differ in their opinions of NCT use and the extent to which they conceive of the blurring of boundaries as personally problematic. Just as individuals consciously interrupt their work or personal life to check email or messages, they may choose to reduce, avoid or resist being constantly connected and overloaded with information. These active choices of managing connectivity are subject to several factors such as having job autonomy, an organisational culture that does not place expectations of being constantly connected to work, i.e. 'always on', and a manager who understands an employee's goals and priorities, and individual differences such as personality traits and preferences. Active choices to manage or control the use of NCTs, such that individuals can balance their resources to meet their work and personal goals, are defined here as 'E-Resistance'. These connectivity management decisions are agentic acts of disconnection and relevant to knowledge-workers [24]. The following sections discuss the background context on E-Resistance, the theoretical framework underpinning it, the importance of further research on this topic and recommendations for individuals and organisations.

6.2   BACKGROUND ON E-RESISTANCE

A surge of research, designed to understand the behaviours and motivation of individuals who feel the need to manage or control their NCT use, has recently been observed. This research stems from the premise that by limiting access to NCTs individuals can better manage their overall well-being and productivity [14, 25]. Researchers [38] have demonstrated that individuals seek work strategies to negotiate NCT interruptions and distractions that emerge from constant connectivity. Ollier-Malaterre et al. [27] theorised a framework relating online boundary management behaviours with consequences for professional relationships. They proposed that individuals make cognisant choices to manage their personal and professional identities and these behaviours stem from important changes to jobs and life stages. For instance, a recent parent may intentionally decide to minimise their work-based NCT use to spend more time with their new-born. As goals and priorities change these shifts in managing communication strategies may be reversed again depending on an individual's life stage and goals. For example, the 'recent parent' of yesterday may tomorrow want to impress their manager, and therefore may increase their availability to meet the demands of work (because new circumstances mean they need a promotion to meet financial demands of their growing family).

There is a body of academic (as above) and non-academic [1, 23] evidence within work and non-work realms reporting the resistance to, and management of, NCTs, particularly in relation to social media and smartphones. Alongside wider initiatives, a San Francisco-based organisation 'The Centre for Humane Technology' has initiated a 'Join the Time Well Spent' movement recommending small steps to 'take control' of technology. These steps might include downloading an application that shows email messages only on request, turning off notifications or charging devices outside the bedroom. Recent research [31] involved analysing a corpus of LinkedIn comments to build a typology of motivations and behaviours underlying disconnection decisions owing to excessive use of mobile phones. Developing strategies to control NCT use are embraced by policymakers at an organisational level too. In between 2012 and 2014, on the behest of labour councils, Volkswagen and BMW banned work-related use of communicative devices after working hours.

Interestingly, the shift from 'flexible' to 'agile' worker is two directional [12]. On the one hand, organisations need to adapt to the rapidly changing demands of globalisation and require their employees to be agile in adapting to these changes. On the other hand, workers will need to anticipate, develop and cope with a range of skills to work in an agile environment. Individuals will need resources that enable learning along with proactively absorbing new knowledge through 'self-flexibility' [33]. Individual reflexivity, where one constantly reflects, examines and subsequently transforms themselves and their behaviours to adapt to the changes, is especially important for individuals as they learn to make dynamic choices to create self-narratives that fit workplace demands and personal goals [33]. Such approaches can enable individuals, organisations and policymakers to drive change so that technology is realigned to meet humanity's best interest. More research is required to understand if and why individuals desire to disconnect. More importantly, it is necessary to understand if these agentic disconnection decisions are supported by the organisational culture, the line manager and the worker's own resolve.

6.3   WHY RESEARCH E-RESISTANCE?

As noted, research on the E-Resistance of work-based communication tools is required, to build on more generic reports relating to how people are resisting (in particular) work-based NCTs. However, research also needs to ask: Who are these E-resistors? What behaviours are they engaging in? Why are they e-resisting? When do they e-resist (life stage)? What is the impact of E-Resistance on well-being and productivity? Will organisations support resistance decisions and build environments to encourage and empower such choices in this agile working age?

Scholarly research on *work-based* NCT resistance is scarce. This unique research gap will potentially contribute to an understanding that fosters a work environment whereby everyone can thrive and reduce the pressures of a constantly connected culture. Importantly, this focus does not warrant a rejection of NCTs. Instead, by answering the questions posed above, research calls for better management of work-based NCT use, such that individuals can participate in intentional and supported acts of withdrawal from NCT use as and when it is deemed necessary [19]. The eventual goal to such a research focus is to enable workers to craft a life where dynamic use and non-use of NCTs can help balance resources to correspond more closely to life events, circumstances, preferences, goals, desires and values.

The brief review above implies that resistance to NCTs is possibly an increasingly distinct, active and agentic phenomenon and not just a mere negation of adoption. Further research can help produce an operationalisation of 'E-resistors'. For instance, an enthusiast of work-based NCT may choose to lower their use for the first time (depending on circumstances) making them 'new rejectors'; someone who has always used work-based NCT sparingly could be a 'native low user'. Moreover, rejection may not apply in its entirety, but may differ in terms of its type (e.g. partial or full), mode (e.g. email, Skype, social media), intensity (e.g. active or passive) and therefore needs detailed understanding. Users may cope with constant connectivity by choosing to temporarily withdraw or completely avoid work-based NCTs at certain times. Users may choose to filter information based on goal hierarchy, sender's status, etc. The assumption of resistance or avoidance of work-based NCTs is not due to inaccessibility or dysfunctionality. It is about users making an informed choice to control work-based NCT use, which can be achieved via constructive tools, infrastructure and support.

A range of individual, social, cultural and organisational factors enable the resistance of work-based NCTs. It is beyond this chapter's scope to explore all factors that explain if and why people resist work-based NCTs. Nonetheless, the above assumption that there are different types of E-resistors highlights the importance of assessing individual differences that drive resistance. These might include availability of resources (e.g. cognitive overload), change in circumstances (e.g. starting a new business) and change in goals (e.g. wanting more family time). Such factors are likely to empower the decision of avoiding, rejecting or reducing work-based NCT use. It can be contended that these circumstances, goals and available resources may change at different periods in time. Broadly speaking, Lifespan Theories [2] and Conservation of Resources (COR) theory [15] support the notion that developmental life stages and available resources potentially direct individuals to manage their work-based NCT use in a manner where they may be consciously controlling work-based NCT use to maintain productivity and overall well-being. Keeping that in mind the following section will discuss the importance of theoretical frameworks that will form the foundation of the research on E-Resistance.

6.4   THEORETICAL FRAMEWORKS SUPPORTING E-RESISTANCE

6.4.1   *How Does Life Stage Affect E-Resistance?*

Understanding different life stages that influence motivations and behaviours to fulfil goals and maintain values is best viewed through the lens of Lifespan Theory [4] when related to E-Resistance. This meta-theory adopts the perspective that patterns in behavioural change occur throughout life and are idiosyncratic. A key aspect of this theory states that individuals will gain and lose resources as a consequence of these developmental processes [3]. The theories assume that individuals proactively manage loss or gain of resources by self-regulation and goal-selection processes to adapt and cope with biological, social, psychological and historical changes that come with different life stages and that they are individualistic [3, 9]. Recently, the author conducted a qualitative interview-based study to understand the behaviour and motivations of E-resistors. Participants ($N = 20$) indicated how some of their NCT use choices were based on goals and resources that vary at different points in life. The following quote suggests that the participant decided to take control of (self-regulate) their work-based NCT use based on their experiences abroad. Individual preferences may affect when and how technology is accessed. In the case below the preference was to reduce evenings spent on NCT use; however, in other cases evening work may offer flexibility to manage non-work situations, such as childcare.

> So, I worked abroad for, um, for, for a number of years (in Asia) and I came back to the UK and I made a very conscious decision when I started working back here. I was not going to start getting into the habit of being on my emails at eight o'clock at night and always being there to respond. Historically I've done that for years.

Lifespan theories share the view that flexible management of developmental process necessitates appropriate mechanisms for distribution and Conservation of Resources [29]. For instance, of the various lifespan theories, Selection, Optimisation and Compensation (SOC) [4] theory postulates that obtaining, retaining and allocating resources change systematically throughout the lifespan. Theory and research explain that during our younger age, resources allocation is largely guided by growth-related goals [3, 8]; however, there is a shift in resource allocation towards sustaining resilience during older age. It would be myopic to accept that age alone determines the resource allocation in this technologically advanced world. Rather, the decision to control or resist NCT use may be based on immediate and long-term circumstances and goals that impact well-being and/or productivity. For instance, another participant from the above study reported a range of strategies to manage their NCT use, indicating that often their life stage or job role and other work-related circumstances determined their work-based NCTs to disturb them out of work hours.

> So, if I was more senior, I'd definitely be having [NCTs] on my phone. Definitely be looking at my emails more. Because I'm more accountable.

The above comment reflects the idea that people may not always follow the same strategy for use or non-use of work-based NCTs. An active choice not to set up work-email on the smartphone could be the right thing to do 'now' but could change if a worker were more senior in their career. Therefore, strategies to control or resist NCTs may change according to available resources, current goals and priorities.

Although a full review of lifespan theory is not viable in this chapter, it can be said that *resources* play an important role in managing the demands of working with NCT in an agile environment depending on one's current circumstances. This notion of resource allocation and management is closely aligned with the COR theory [15] discussed below. Together they contribute to the conceptual framework of work-based E-Resistance, being developed by the author.

6.5   How Conservation of Resources (COR) Theory Can Address E-Resistance

As reviewed above, lifespan theories are based on the fundamental assumption that developmental processes are directed by gains and losses of resources at every life stage [2]. Resources can come in the form of personal characteristics (e.g. conscientiousness), conditions (e.g. parenthood), energy (e.g. sleep) or objects (e.g. smartphones), that help people to achieve their goals [13, 15]. Resource loss can lead to stress and strain, mitigated by the use of coping mechanisms (e.g. self-regulation and goal selection) to protect from losses, and to gain or replenish lost resources [16]. Largely speaking, resources enable goal attainment [10] and a resource must be defined in context to a specific goal [13]. However, having access to goal-relevant resources does not automatically lead to goal attainment. Resources can be utilised cautiously or indiscreetly. For instance, autonomy is considered a resource in the workplace, nonetheless if invested imprudently it can be considered volatile [34] as it offers flexibility but is also intrusive [35]. Therefore, resource management, aligned with goals and values, is vital for successful development and overall well-being. Understandably, resources play a pivotal role in managing stress associated with work-based NCT use and consequently, individuals exercise agency to manage their resources (e.g. acts of resistance) to maintain optimum functioning.

A fundamental tenet of COR theory is that 'individuals strive to obtain, retain, foster and protect things they centrally value' [16, p. 104]. COR stresses that individuals have an 'evolutionary-based built-in' and 'powerful bias' to emphasise resource loss and minimise resource gain. Therefore, resource loss (e.g. lower productivity) is more salient than resource gain (e.g. impression management) suggesting that work-based NCT losses will have more impact than corresponding gains. Another key tenet of COR is resource loss and gain spirals. It suggests that an initial loss (e.g. lower attention span) in personal resources owing to contextual demands (e.g. interruptions) induces additional losses (e.g. loss of productivity) since there are fewer resources available to deal effectively with chronic demands (e.g. constant connectivity) or to collect contextual resources (e.g. supervisor or client approval). Hobfoll et al. [17] suggest one way to cope with strain and encourage stress resistance is to break the iteration of loss spiral by investing in resource gain spirals. From an E-resistors viewpoint 'switching off' work-related NCTs after working hours could help individuals to renew their lost resources and increase their well-being [32].

COR theory is, perhaps, one of the most noteworthy theories explaining stress and well-being and is closely aligned with lifespan development theories [16]. Together they offer a useful theoretical foundation to understand work-based E-Resistance.

6.6   Significance of Understanding E-Resistance

Through this review and ongoing study, it is intended that stakeholders can understand the causes and consequences of actively managing work-based NCT use. Understanding E-Resistance can potentially support the effort towards a more balanced use of work-based NCTs that is aligned with an individual's life goals and overall well-being. Academically, most research in the field of resistance to NCTs is within the realms of social media and smartphone usage. Advancing this field, this research offers a unique contribution towards the under-researched area of work-based NCT resistance. Additionally, the findings will contribute to the literature on Lifespan and COR theories. From a practical standpoint, exploring work-based NCT resistance can potentially help in designing NCTs to improve interaction with its users (e.g. non-extracting) and increase productivity (e.g. less errors in tasks). This research can encourage individuals and policymakers to consider how connectivity management can be structured to follow personal alignments and decision styles. It is anticipated that an organisational culture that allows 'real' autonomy and agency to manage connectivity can foster effective remote working relationships that are increasingly common in an agile workplace.

Based on the evidence from the author's exploratory study (above) on E-Resistance, Table 6.1 offers recommendations for managing or controlling work-based NCT use.

Table 6.1 Recommendations for individuals and organisations on managing work-based NCTs

For individuals	For organisations
Communicate NCT preferences to your colleagues, manager, clients and family	Embed training on work-based NCT use as part of the on-boarding process
Be aware of temporary increases in work-based NCT use and avoid making that the new norm	Provide regular talks and training on how to manage NCTs (awareness)
Personalise notification settings when introduced to NCTs at work and check alter them if required	Managers should notice any behavioural changes towards NCT use and empower workers to have conversations about managing these
Respect your colleagues' preferences of NCT use and accessibility	Develop an organisational culture of not being constantly connected and creating a safe space for employees to have a voice and 'real' agency over their connectivity management
Develop self-reflexivity to match and prioritise NCT use with goals at work and outside	Embrace and endorse individual differences in NCT use

6.7   CONCLUSION

This chapter highlights the need to understand E-Resistance and management of work-based NCTs and the impact this might have on individuals. Managers can be proactive in empowering their employees to make active choices about their work-based NCT use, such that they can balance their personal and professional goals. Understanding this behaviour may help individuals and organisations to carve their own digital philosophies in alignment with one's goals and values in their personal and professional life and an increasingly agile working world.

REFERENCES

1. Anderson, J., & Rainie, L. (2018). *The future of well-being in a tech-saturated world*. Pew Research Center. https://www.pewresearch.org/int ernet/2018/04/17/the-future-of-well-being-in-a-tech-saturated-world/. Accessed 15 January 2020.
2. Baltes, P. B. (1987). Theoretical propositions of life-span developmental psychology: On the dynamics between growth and decline. *Developmental Psychology, 23*(5), 611–626. https://doi.org/10.1037/0012-1649. 23.5.611.

3. Baltes, P. B., & Baltes, M. M. (1990). Psychological perspectives on successful aging: The model of selective optimization with compensation. In P. B. Baltes & M. M. Baltes (Eds.), *Successful aging: Perspectives from the behavioral sciences* (pp. 1–34). New York: Cambridge University Press. https://doi.org/10.1017/CBO9780511665684.003.

4. Cousins, K., & Robey, D. (2015). Managing work-life boundaries with mobile technologies: An interpretive study of mobile work practices. *Information Technology and People, 28*(1), 34–71. https://doi.org/10.1108/ITP-08-2013-0155.

5. Demerouti, E., Derks, D., Lieke, L., & Bakker, A. B. (2014). New ways of working: Impact on working conditions, work-family balance, and well-being. In C. Korunka & P. Hoonakker (Eds.), *The impact of ICT on quality of working life* (pp. 123–141). Dordrecht: Springer.

6. Dos Santos, B., & Sussman, L. (2000). Improving the return on IT investment: The productivity paradox. *International Journal of Information Management, 20*(6), 429–431. https://doi.org/10.1016/S0268-4012(00)00037-2.

7. Dulebohn, J. H., & Hoch, J. E. (2017). Virtual teams in organizations. *Human Resource Management Review, 27*(4), 569–574. https://doi.org/10.1016/j.hrmr.2016.12.004.

8. Ebner, N. C., Freund, A. M., & Baltes, P. B. (2006). Developmental changes in personal goal orientation from young to late adulthood: From striving for gains to maintenance and prevention of losses. *Psychology and Aging, 21*(4), 664–678. https://doi.org/10.1037/0882-7974.21.4.664.

9. Featherman, D. L. (1983). Life-span perspectives in social science research. In P. B. Baltes & O. G. Brim (Eds.), *Life-span development and behaviour* (pp. 1–57). New York: Academic Press.

10. Freund, A. M., & Riediger, M. (2001). What I have and what I do: The role of resource loss and gain throughout life. *Applied Psychology: An International Review, 50*(3), 370–380. https://psycnet.apa.org/doi/10.1111/1464-0597.00063.

11. Garrett, R. K., & Danziger, J. N. (2008). IM = Interruption management? Instant messaging and disruption in the workplace. *Journal of Computer-Mediated Communication, 13*(1), 23–42. https://doi.org/10.1111/j.1083-6101.2007.00384.x.

12. Gillies, D. (2011). Agile bodies: A new imperative in neoliberal governance. *Journal of Education Policy, 26*(2), 207–223. https://doi.org/10.1080/02680939.2010.508177.

13. Halbesleben, J. R., Neveu, J. P., Paustian-Underdahl, S. C., & Westman, M. (2014). Getting to the "COR": Understanding the role of resources in Conservation of Resources theory. *Journal of Management, 40*(5), 1334–1364. https://doi.org/10.1177/0149206314527130.

14. Hesselberth, P. (2018). Discourses on disconnectivity and the right to disconnect. *New Media and Society*, *20*(5), 1994–2010. https://doi.org/10.1177/1461444817711449.

15. Hobfoll, S. E. (1989). Conservation of resources: A new attempt at conceptualizing stress. *American Psychologist*, *44*(3), 513–524. https://doi.org/10.1037/0003-066X.44.3.513.

16. Hobfoll, S. E. (2002). Social and psychological resources and adaptation. *Review of General Psychology*, *6*(4), 307–324. https://doi.org/10.1037/1089-2680.6.4.307.

17. Hobfoll, S. E., Halbesleben, J. R., Neveu, J. P., & Westman, M. (2018). Conservation of resources in the organizational context: The reality of resources and their consequences. *Annual Review of Organizational Psychology and Organizational Behaviour*, *5*, 103–128. https://doi.org/10.1146/annurev-orgpsych-032117-104640.

18. Jackson, T. W., Dawson, R., & Wilson, D. (2003). Understanding email interaction increases organizational productivity. *Communications of the ACM*, *46*(8), 80–84. https://doi.org/10.1145/859670.859673.

19. Kolb, D. G., Caza, A., & Collins, P. D. (2012). States of connectivity: New questions and new directions'. *Organization Studies*, *33*(2), 267–273. https://doi.org/10.1177/0170840611431653.

20. Korunka, C., & Hoonakker, P. L. T. (2014). The future of ICT and quality of working life: Challenges, Benefits, and risks. In C. Korunka & P. Hoonakker (Eds.), *The impact of ICT on quality of working life* (pp. 205–219). Dordrecht: Springer.

21. Kushlev, K., & Dunn, E. W. (2015). Checking email less frequently can reduce stress. *Computers in Human Behaviour*, *43*, 220–228. https://doi.org/10.1016/j.chb.2014.11.005.

22. Levy, D. M. (2007). No time to think: Reflections on information technology and contemplative scholarship. *Ethics and Information Technology*, *9*(4), 237–249. https://doi.org/10.1007/s10676-007-9142-6.

23. Lyons, K. (2015, June 27). *Turn off, tune out: National Unplugging Day hopes to give Britain a digital detox*. Guardian. https://www.theguardian.com/technology/2015/jun/27/turn-off-tune-out-national-unplugging-day-hopes-to-give-britain-a-digital-detox. Accessed 5 February 2020.

24. Mazmanian, M., Orlikowski, W. J., & Yates, J. (2013). The autonomy paradox: The implications of mobile email devices for knowledge professionals. *Organization Science*, *24*(5), 1337–1357. https://doi.org/10.1287/orsc.1120.0806.

25. Morandin, G., Russo, M., & Ollier-Malaterre, A. (2018). Put down that phone! Smart use of Smartphones for work and beyond. *Journal of Management Inquiry*, *27*(3), 325–356. https://doi.org/10.1177/1056492618762964.

26. Mullan, K., & Wajcman, J. (2017). Have mobile devices changed working patterns in the 21st century? A time-diary analysis of work extension in the UK. *Work, Employment & Society, 33*(1), 3–20. https://doi.org/10.1177/0950017017730529.
27. Ollier-Malaterre, A., Rothard, N. P., & Berg, J. M. (2013). When worlds collide in cyberspace: How boundary work in social networks impacts personal relationships. *Academy of Management Review, 38*(4), 645–669. https://doi.org/10.5465/amr.2011.0235.
28. Park, Y., & Jex, S. M. (2011). Work–home boundary management using communication and information technology. *International Journal of Stress Management, 18*(2), 133–152. https://doi.org/10.1037/a0022759.
29. Riediger, M., Li, S.-C., & Lindenberger, U. (2006). Selection, optimization, and compensation as developmental mechanisms of adaptive resource allocation: Review and preview. In J. E. Birren & K. W. Schaire (Eds.), *Handbook of the psychology of aging* (pp. 289–313). Amsterdam, Netherlands: Elsevier.
30. Rothbard, N. P., Phillips, K. W., & Dumas, T. L. (2005). Managing multiple roles: Work-family policies and individuals desire for segmentation. *Organization Science, 16*(3), 243–258. https://doi.org/10.1287/orsc.1050.0124.
31. Russo, M., Ollier-Malaterre, A., & Morandin, G. (2019). Breaking out from constant connectivity: Agentic regulation of smartphone use. *Computers in Human Behavior, 98*, 11–19. https://doi.org/10.1016/j.chb.2019.03.038.
32. Sonnentag, S., & Bayer, U. V. (2005). Switching off mentally: Predictors and consequences of psychological detachment from work during off-job time. *Journal of Occupational Health Psychology, 10*(4), 393–414. https://doi.org/10.1037/1076-8998.10.4.393.
33. Swan, E., & Fox, S. (2009). Becoming flexible: Self-flexibility and its pedagogies. *British Journal of Management, 20*(1), 149–159. https://doi.org/10.1111/j.1467-8551.2008.00642.x.
34. ten Brummelhuis, L. L., & Bakker, A. B. (2012). A resource perspective on the work-home interface. *American Psychologist, 67*(7), 545–556. https://doi.org/10.1037/a0027974.
35. Towers, I., Duxbury, L., Higgins, C., & Thomas, J. (2006). Time thieves and space invaders: Technology, work, and the organization. *Journal of Organizational Change Management, 19*(5), 593–618. https://doi.org/10.1108/09534810610686076.
36. Volkmer, S. A., & Lermer, E. (2019). Unhappy and addicted to your phone?—Higher mobile phone use is associated with lower well-being. *Computers in Human Behaviour, 93*, 210–219. https://doi.org/10.1016/j.chb.2018.12.015.

37. Wajcman, J., Bittman, M., & Brown, J. E. (2008). Families without borders: Mobile phones, connectedness, and work-home divisions. *Sociology, 42*(4), 635–652. https://doi.org/10.1177/0038038508091620.
38. Wajcman, J., & Rose, E. (2011). Constant connectivity: Rethinking interruptions at work. *Organization Studies, 32*(7), 941–961. https://doi.org/10.1177/0170840611410829.
39. Wayne, J. H., Butts, M. M., Casper, W. J., & Allen, T. A. (2017). In search of balance: A conceptual and empirical integration of multiple meanings of work-family balance. *Personnel Psychology, 70*(1), 167–210. https://doi.org/10.1111/peps.12132.

PART IV

Healthy, Effective and Sustainable Agile Working

CHAPTER 7

A Review of the Agile Working Literature in Relation to Five Facets of Well-Being

Maria Charalampous

Abstract This chapter reviews the impact that work conducted anywhere, at any time using technology, has on individuals' well-being at work. Well-being is examined in terms of five key dimensions, relating to (i) affective, (ii) cognitive, (iii) social, (iv) professional and (v) psychosomatic experiences pertaining to an agile working context. The chapter draws upon the existing literature concerning agile working practices—specifically in relation to 'always on' remote work and examines these in relation to the five dimensions of well-being. The beneficial impact of agile working on employee satisfaction, commitment and positive emotions is acknowledged, along with potential drawbacks, such as social and professional isolation, and perceived threats to professional advancement. Research oversights in relation to cognitive, professional and psychosomatic factors are highlighted. Implications for practice are then discussed, with appropriate interventions and strategies suggested.

M. Charalampous (✉)
Coventry University, Coventry, UK
e-mail: ac2821@coventry.ac.uk

Keywords Agile working · Remote work · E-work · Telework ·
Always-on culture · Well-being

7.1   INTRODUCTION

The way that individuals work has profoundly changed, especially with
the advent of an exponential increase in Information and Communication
Technology (ICT) use [14, 28]. European statistics indicate that, thanks
to modern technology, 3% of working individuals in 2015 were predominantly working from home, with 10% doing so occasionally [14]. In the
USA, the number of employees working remotely moved from 39 to 43%
between 2012 and 2016 [18]. Using ICTs to work in an agile and flexible
way has been found to be of increasing value to employees, who cite this
as a key reason that attracts them to organisations that offer such flexibility [21]. Considering the COVID-19 pandemic (as announced by the
World Health Organisation in March 2020) remote e-working practices
were implemented by many organisations across the world, to reduce the
spread of the virus [31]. In Chapter 1, it was indicated that almost half of
office workers are now working from home during the COVID-19 crisis.

Notwithstanding the undeniable growth of agile working practices,
facilitated by ICTs, there is no consensus as to its precise impact on
individuals' well-being, with scholars presenting both positive and negative viewpoints. For example, whereas agile workers' well-being can
be enhanced through improved work-life balance, greater control and
enhanced communications, it could be harmed through increased digital
interruptions induced by location flexibility [38]. Whilst individuals
report greater positive emotions (affect) on the days they work from home
[2], agile working also has the potential for workers to become socially
and professionally isolated [6, 20]. Agile workers in one study claimed
that being 'out of sight' felt like they were also 'out of mind' [36].

The ICT use that accompanies agile working also affords workers
the opportunity to engage in out-of-contract work during evenings and
weekends [35]. Schlachter et al.'s (2018) review of 56 studies revealed
that some organisations encourage individuals to engage in an always
on culture, where a vicious 'cycle of responsiveness' is maintained by
colleagues and managers [12]. In agile working, individuals are enabled
to work at any time and any given location, which per se increases
the likelihood of using ICTs, and simultaneously has been found to

increase job-related characteristics of control, flexibility and efficiency [17]. Hence, the more the autonomy that agile workers may have, the greater effort and hours are likely to be put into their work [23]. This work intensification has been found to adversely impact workers' well-being [35]. In particular, using ICTs outside of contracted work hours can lead to a greater blurring of boundaries and work-life interference, increasing individuals' need for recovery from work [22], and harming their psychological and physiological well-being [35]. Given these recent trends, it is now timely to examine the potential paradoxes in the relationship between agile working and employee well-being [1, 11].

7.2   A MULTIDIMENSIONAL APPROACH TO AGILE WORKING AND WELL-BEING AT WORK

Agile working has a multifaceted impact on individuals' working and personal lives [1]. As such, remote e-working (an agile working practice—see Chapter 2) 'can and should be studied from a variety of theoretical perspectives and frameworks' [4, p. 116]. Adopting a multidimensional approach is highly relevant, as it provides a meaningful contextual framework for discussing and elucidating the relationship between agile working and well-being at work [9]. A recent systematic review [9], drawing upon Van Horn et al.'s (2004) work-related well-being model [40], suggested that agile workers' well-being can be better understood by considering five distinct dimensions and their subdimensions. These well-being dimensions are: (i) affective—including emotions, job satisfaction, organisational commitment and emotional exhaustion; (ii) cognitive—capturing difficulties in concentrating and taking in new information; (iii) social—including relationships with colleagues and supervisors, and experiences of isolation; (iv) professional—consisting of autonomy, competence and career development; and lastly, (v) psychosomatic—comprising musculoskeletal and fatigue symptoms.

In the review [9], utilising 63 studies and 37,553 working individuals, the authors indicated how these well-being dimensions were intertwined, providing a deeper understanding of the impact of agile work. For example, both decreased emotional exhaustion and increased job satisfaction (affective dimensions) that individuals experienced were enabled when the level of autonomy (professional dimension) was higher [17, 34]. Furthermore, experiencing good working relationships (social dimension) was related to individuals being more committed to their work (affective dimension) [15]. Receiving support from both the organisation (social dimension) in general, and more specifically related to agile working, reduced psychological strain (affective dimension) and social isolation (social dimension) and increased job satisfaction (affective dimension) [37]. Such findings suggest that, rather than solitude leading to social isolation, isolation appears to benefit some individuals, potentially because they are able to filter out office-based distractions and focus on specific tasks that require concentration [16]. Investigating the interactions between the five well-being dimensions can allow for more criticality when understanding agile workers' well-being. The sections below examine these distinct well-being dimensions in more depth.

7.3 The Positive Impact of Agile Working on Individuals

Organisational studies have mainly discussed the positive impact of agile working on individuals' well-being, in relation to affective dimensions, including job satisfaction [15], organisational commitment, [11] reduced stress levels and reduced emotional exhaustion levels [32]. These positive benefits have been attributed to agile working practices affording more flexible working, the avoidance of commuting, enabling better management of work and personal life demands, and a greater sense of organisational support [23].

It also appears that personal preferences for agile working practices may impact affective well-being experiences, although there is a scarcity of research relating to this. Nevertheless, studies have found that employees who: are more open to experience, ruminate less, prefer virtual (compared to face-to-face) teamwork and have more social connections outside their workplace experience greater positive emotions when working remotely [2]. Moreover, 'workaholic' (high level of work drive and a low level of work enjoyment) individuals were found to be more satisfied with their job when working away from the main office location [27] compared to office-based colleagues. For individuals with greater discretion and control over their job tasks and ICT use, the negative impact of ICT use on well-being is reduced [35]. Such findings indicate that organisations who provide support to employees and acknowledge that there is no 'one size fits all' approach to agile working are likely to observe greater benefits to employees' well-being. Applying more research attention to the concepts of working preferences and personality types is now required to foresee how agile working is suited to individuals with different styles. Chapter 4 provides further insights into this under-researched area.

Autonomy has also been suggested as one of the key resources provided by agile working, which appears to increase workers' positive affectivity [17, 38] and reduce emotional exhaustion [32]. This contradicts the 'autonomy paradox', which has suggested that the greater freedom individuals have around their work, especially because of the available ICTs, the greater the work intensification (feeling controlled and restricted by work) [29, 33].

7.4 REMOTE E-WORKING AND THE FEAR OF BEING FORGOTTEN: SOCIAL AND PROFESSIONAL ISOLATION

One of the most discussed drawbacks regarding agile working practices is the social isolation that may be experienced through remote working [29]. Missed developmental opportunities, interpersonal networking and informal learning, which are easily accessible in an office setting, contribute to feelings of isolation, potentially to the detriment of job satisfaction [10] and performance [20]. Scholars have suggested that working from locations different to the office can occasionally be perceived as an equivalent of workplace absence [30]. These findings, consequently, raise the question about whether constant visibility is a fundamental ingredient to career progression and success.

Feelings of isolation and frustration were mitigated when remote e-workers relied on synchronous methods (e.g. mobile phones) to communicate with colleagues [24]. One potential reason is that the mobile phone (as opposed to email or other text-based ICT) is regarded as a medium that provides richness of communication, enabling immediate feedback, actual vocal and visual contact, using natural language communication. Further, organisations that promote a culture of employee support have been found to implement remote e-working practices more effectively [25], and more positively influence individuals' job satisfaction, commitment and engagement whilst reducing psychological strain and social isolation [5, 15]. Organisational support can be observed via practices such as providing technical support and the resources to enable remote e-working, implementing new information technology systems when needed and trusting employees when are not physically present in an office [5].

7.5   UNDERDEVELOPED DIMENSIONS
IN UNDERSTANDING AGILE WORKING AND WELL-BEING

The author's recent systematic review [9] demonstrated good evidence for agile working factors likely to impact affective and social well-being components but revealed a gap in knowledge relating to the cognitive, professional and psychosomatic well-being dimensions. Firstly, in relation to the cognitive dimension, it appears that individuals choose to work away from their company's offices in an attempt to eliminate distractions and concentrate better [32]. Concentration could be impaired however by an increase in receipt of electronic interruptions [26]. Constant connectivity also means that agile workers may be more susceptible to failures to mentally detach from work [7]. To provide greater insight, the author attempted to further investigate whether cognitive processes contribute to the experience of well being from agile working, especially in relation to concentration and recovery [8]. Qualitative findings, based on 40 employees working in a British IT company, showed that a key factor in ameliorating cognitive weariness from agile working was choosing to do 'the right thing at the right place' (e.g. tasks demanding concentration may be best undertaken in a home environment). Further, blocking e-distractions—to prevent agile workers from becoming cognitively fatigued—was revealed to be key [8]. Adding to these findings, a cross-sectional study within 399 remote e-workers [8] suggested that the more individuals detach from their work, the more positive their mental health is, and cognitive weariness also reduces. Technology overload and complexity (technostress) predicts cognitive weariness at such times.

In relation to the professional dimension, limited research suggests that workers can feel professionally stunted when absent from physical office space [10]. However, career prospects are not necessarily hampered by this. A meta-analysis [17] showed that agile workers do not perceive diminished career prospects, when compared with their office-based colleagues. In samples with a higher percentage of women, perceptions of positive career prospects in agile working contexts were stronger, indicating the enabling role of agile working to women's careers [17]. Recent literature identifies a number of factors that can positively contribute to agile workers' career progression perceptions. Particularly, at an individual level, agile workers are encouraged to be proactive by being in contact with members of the organisation, who are important to their career; making themselves seen [8]. Having managers who are approachable, who set clear expectations and make contact beyond work-related matters is also important as keeping in touch becomes even more critical in an agile working setting [8]. At an organisational level, a supportive and inclusive culture seems to be essential [25, 19].

Systematic review findings [9] have also explored the notion of professional competence (i.e. relating to knowledge, skills and attitudes), and research suggests that individuals' perceptions of competence can assist them in developing their careers in agile working environments. Very recent qualitative data proposed that a competent agile worker should primarily be self-disciplined [8]. The fact that office cues are not present anymore increases the importance of staying focused and self-motivated. Good communication skills, especially when using electronic means, were also proposed to be key to getting effective messages across. Choosing the right electronic medium was perceived as very important, with a great need to overcome individuals' overreliance on email communication. More detail is now required in terms of how different levels of competence can impact career development and professional progression, when engaged in agile working.

Finally, there have been calls for psychosomatic conditions to be better understood, in relation to agile working [9, 14]. Agile workers are exposed to different ergonomic risks compared to their office-based colleagues; for example, they may lack access to ergonomically designed working environments [13] and potentially be susceptible to a more sedentary lifestyle, which can be damaging to individuals' health [3]. The long hours of work, which are exacerbated in some agile working practices [23], can harm individuals' health [2].

More research in this area is now of fundamental importance, ensuring that work environments are ergonomically designed and guidance is in place for agile workers, thus reducing physical issues and complaints [39]. Linking to psychosomatic health [1], a question is raised as to whether agile working can affect health-related behaviours (e.g. eating habits, exercise habits and breaks). Decreased exercise coupled with sedentary working, and a poorer diet may lead to a decline in an individual's health outcomes [39]. In the absence of evidence, links between psychosomatic well-being at work and agile working cannot be conclusive, restricting our complete understanding on the topic. Chapter 8 deals with several of these issues in more depth.

7.6   WHAT CAN ORGANISATIONS
AND PRACTITIONERS DO?

The existing literature can inform organisational practices and strategies, to safeguard agile workers' well-being. Organisations are advised to foster a supportive and trusting organisational culture (e.g. eradicating micro-management, focusing on outputs) for agile working, where individuals feel comfortable conducting work outside an office location. Supervision practices, which instil relationship-building, provide social support and encourage face-to-face interaction, should also be considered as a means for reducing social and professional isolation. As certain tasks are best achieved in isolation, and others in a social setting, organisations can encourage agile workers to work away from an office location when they need to concentrate, but to physically co-locate with colleagues for tasks requiring teamwork, social interaction and brainstorming [8]. When agile working involves working full-time remotely, the organisation should focus on helping remote e-workers maintain connections with colleagues via face-to-face gatherings and social events.

To manage the 'always on' culture and its embedded social norms and expectations for being constantly available, organisations are encouraged to openly discuss non-working hours ICT use. This will allow the development of practices that help agile workers to manage home and work boundaries in a way that best suits them and the organisational needs. Personal preferences regarding ICT use, individuals' perceptions of their own use and expectations to respond to communications need to be identified. For example, organisations might consider circulating weekly email tips for promoting well-being via good digital practice. Relevant advice could encourage individuals to observe good email etiquette, and ensure they have time each day where they disconnect.

7.7   LIMITATIONS IN THE FIELD
AND IMPLICATIONS FOR FUTURE RESEARCH

A multidimensional approach provides a greater understanding of how different well-being dimensions are intertwined. Simultaneously, well-being dimensions, which have been overlooked to date, need to be explored further, and the five dimensions framework provides a useful way of categorising where these gaps are. As seen, this is especially relevant in relation to the cognitive, professional and psychosomatic well-being dimensions.

7.8   Conclusion

Agile working impacts individuals' well-being at work. This impact appears to be multifaceted and complex. Effectively collating evidence in relation to five key dimensions of well-being allows researchers to capture a more vigorous understanding of agile workers' well-being at work, specifically in regard to the 'always on' remote working nature of agile working. The present chapter highlights a number of areas for future research, which would allow for a greater understanding of the impact that agile working has on individuals. This includes exploring cognitive weariness individuals may experience, especially as a result of ICT use invading personal and work lives and decreasing switching off from work. Psychosomatic health and lifestyle habits need to also be more greatly considered. It is also clearly indicated that agile working's true purpose is about allowing individuals to operate in ways that suit them. This suggests that if individuals can be educated and informed about how to optimise their own effectiveness, then the future of agile working is very promising.

References

1. Allen, T. D., Golden, T. D., & Shockley, K. M. (2015). How effective is telecommuting? Assessing the status of our scientific findings. *Psychological Science in the Public Interest, 16*(2), 40–68. https://doi.org/10.1177/152 9100615593273.

2. Anderson, A. J., Kaplan, S. A., & Vega, R. P. (2015). The impact of telework on emotional experience: When, and for whom, does telework improve daily affective well-being? *European Journal of Work and Organizational Psychology, 24*(6), 882–897. https://doi.org/10.1080/1359432X. 2014.966086.

3. Bannai, A., & Tamakoshi, A. (2014). The association between long working hours and health: A systematic review of epidemiological evidence. *Scandinavian Journal of Work, Environment & Health, 40*(1), 5–18. https://doi. org/10.5271/sjweh.3388.

4. Baruch, Y. (2001). The status of research on teleworking and an agenda for future research. *International Journal of Management Reviews, 3*(2), 113–129. https://doi.org/10.1111/1468-2370.00058.

5. Bentley, T. A., Teo, S. T. T., McLeod, L., Tan, F., Bosua, R., & Gloet, M. (2016). The role of organisational support in teleworker well-being: A socio-technical systems approach. *Applied Ergonomics, 52*, 207–215. https://doi. org/10.1016/j.apergo.2015.07.019.

6. Boell, S. K., Cecez-Kecmanovic, D., & Campbell, J. (2016). Telework paradoxes and practices: The importance of the nature of work. *New Technology, Work and Employment, 31*(2), 114–131. https://doi.org/10.1111/ntwe.12063.

7. Braukmann, J., Schmitt, A., Ďuranová, L., & Ohly, S. (2018). Identifying ICT-related affective events across life domains and examining their unique relationships with employee recovery. *Journal of Business and Psychology, 33*(4), 529–544. https://doi.org/10.1007/s10869-017-9508-7.

8. Charalampous, M., Grant, C. A., & Tramontano, C. (2020). *The development of the e-work well-being scale and further validation of the e-work life scale.* Unpublished doctoral thesis, Coventry University.

9. Charalampous, M., Grant, C. A., Tramontano, C., & Michailidis, E. (2019). Systematically reviewing remote e-workers' well-being at work: A multidimensional approach. *European Journal of Work and Organizational Psychology, 28*(1), 51–73. https://doi.org/10.1080/1359432X.2018.1541886.

10. Cooper, C. D., & Kurland, N. B. (2002). Telecommuting, professional isolation, and employee development in public and private organizations. *Journal of Organizational Behavior, 23*(4), 511–532. https://doi.org/10.1002/job.145.

11. De Menezes, L. M., & Kelliher, C. (2011). Flexible working and performance: A systematic review of the evidence for a business case. *International Journal of Management Reviews, 13*(4), 452–474. https://doi.org/10.1111/j.1468-2370.2011.00301.x.

12. Derks, D., Duin, D., Tims, M., & Bakker, A. B. (2015). Smartphone use and work–home interference: The moderating role of social norms and employee work engagement. *Journal of Occupational and Organizational Psychology, 88*(1), 155–177. https://doi.org/10.1111/joop.12083.

13. Ellison, J. K. (2012). Ergonomics for telecommuters and other remote workers. *Professional Safety, 57*(6), 86–90.

14. Eurofound and the International Labour Office. (2017). *Working anytime, anywhere: The effects on the world of work.* Publications Office of the European Union, Luxembourg, and the International Labour Office, Geneva. http://eurofound.link/ef1658. Accessed 10 August 2020.

15. Fay, M. J., & Kline, S. L. (2011). Co-worker relationships and informal communication in high-intensity telecommuting. *Journal of Applied Communication Research, 39*(2), 144–163. https://doi.org/10.1080/00909882.2011.556136.

16. Fonner, K. L., & Roloff, M. E. (2010). Why teleworkers are more satisfied with their jobs than are office-based workers: When less contact is beneficial. *Journal of Applied Communication Research, 38*(4), 336–361. https://doi.org/10.1080/00909882.2010.513998.

17. Gajendran, R. S., & Harrison, D. A. (2007). The good, the bad, and the unknown about telecommuting: Meta-analysis of psychological mediators and individual consequences. *Journal of Applied Psychology, 92*(6), 1524–1541. https://doi.org/10.1037/0021-9010.92.6.1524.
18. Gallup. (2017). *State of the American Workplace Report.* http://www.gallup.com/reports/199961/state-american-workplace-report2017.aspx?ays=n. Accessed 10 August 2020.
19. Gálvez, A., Martínez, M. J., & Pérez, C. (2011). Telework and work-life balance: Some dimensions for organisational change. *Journal of Workplace Rights, 16*(3–4), 273–297. https://doi.org/10.2190/WR.16.3-4.B.
20. Golden, T. D., Veiga, J. F., & Dino, R. N. (2008). The impact of professional isolation on teleworker job performance and turnover intentions: Does time spent teleworking, interacting face-to-face, or having access to communication-enhancing technology matter? *Journal of Applied Psychology, 93*(6), 1412–1421. https://doi.org/10.1037/a0012722.
21. Haines, V. Y., III, St-Onge, S., & Archambault, M. (2002). Environmental and person antecedents of telecommuting outcomes. *Journal of Organizational and End User Computing, 14*(3), 32–50. https://doi.org/10.4018/joeuc.2002070103.
22. Jansen, N., Kant, I., van Amelsvoort, L., Nijhuis, F., & van den Brandt, P. (2003). Need for recovery from work: Evaluating short-term effects of working hours, patterns and schedules. *Ergonomics, 46*(7), 664–680. https://doi.org/10.1080/0014013031000085662.
23. Kelliher, C., & Anderson, D. (2010). Doing more with less? Flexible working practices and the intensification of work. *Human Relations, 63*(1), 83–106. https://doi.org/10.1177/0018726709349199.
24. Lal, B., & Dwivedi, Y. K. (2009). Homeworkers' usage of mobile phones; social isolation in the home-workplace. *Journal of Enterprise Information Management, 22*(3), 257–274. https://doi.org/10.1108/17410390910949715.
25. Lautsch, B. A., Kossek, E. E., & Eaton, S. C. (2009). Supervisory approaches and paradoxes in managing telecommunication implementation. *Human Relations, 62*(6), 795–827. https://doi.org/10.1177/0018726709104543.
26. Leonardi, P. M., Treem, J. W., & Jackson, M. H. (2010). The connectivity paradox: Using technology to both decrease and increase perceptions of distance in distributed work arrangements. *Journal of Applied Communication Research, 38*(1), 85–105. https://doi.org/10.1080/00909880903483599.
27. Luse, A., McElroy, J. C., Townsend, A. M., & Demarie, S. (2013). Personality and cognitive style as predictors of preference for working in virtual

teams. *Computers in Human Behavior, 29*(4), 1825–1832. https://doi.org/10.1016/j.chb.2013.02.007.

28. Maitland, A., & Thomson, P. (2014). *Future Work (Expanded and Updated): Changing organizational culture for the new world of work.* London, UK: Springer.
29. Michel, A. (2011). Transcending socialization: A nine-year ethnography of the body's role in organizational control and knowledge workers' transformation. *Administrative Science Quarterly, 56*(3), 325–368. https://doi.org/10.1177/0001839212437519.
30. Morganson, V. J., Major, D. A., Oborn, K. L., Verive, J. M., & Heelan, M. P. (2010). Comparing telework locations and traditional work arrangements: Differences in work-life balance support, job satisfaction, and inclusion. *Journal of Managerial Psychology, 25*(6), 578–595. https://doi.org/10.1108/02683941011056941.
31. Office for National Statistics. (2020). *Coronavirus and the social impacts on Great Britain: 19 June 2020.* London: Office for National Statistics. https://www.ons.gov.uk/releases/coronavirusandthesocialimpacts ongreatbritain19june2020. Accessed 10 August 2020.
32. Peters, P., & Wildenbeest, M. (2011). Telecommuters: Creative or exhausted workers? A study into the conditions under which telecommuters experience flow and exhaustion. In C. Kelliher & J. Richardson (Eds.), *New ways of organizing work: Developments, perspectives and experiences* (pp. 134–151). New York: Routledge.
33. Putnam, L. L., Myers, K. K., & Gailliard, B. M. (2014). Examining the tensions in workplace flexibility and exploring options for new directions. *Human Relations, 67*(4), 413–440. https://doi.org/10.1177/001872671 3495704.
34. Sardeshmukh, S. R., Sharma, D., & Golden, T. D. (2012). Impact of telework on exhaustion and job engagement: A job demands and job resources model. *New Technology, Work and Employment, 27*(3), 193–207. https://doi.org/10.1111/j.1468-005X.2012.00284.x.
35. Schlachter, S., McDowall, A., Cropley, M., & Inceoglu, I. (2018). Voluntary work-related technology use during non-work time: A narrative synthesis of empirical research and research agenda. *International Journal of Management Reviews, 20*(4), 825–846. https://doi.org/10.1111/ijmr.12165.
36. Sewell, G., & Taskin, L. (2015). Out of sight, out of mind in a new world of work? Autonomy, control, and spatiotemporal scaling in telework. *Organization Studies, 36*(11), 1507–1529. https://doi.org/10.1177/017084061 5593587.
37. Suh, A., & Lee, J. (2017). Understanding teleworkers' technostress and its influence on job satisfaction. *Internet Research, 27*(1), 140–159. https://doi.org/10.1108/IntR-06-2015-0181.

38. Ter Hoeven, C. L., & Van Zoonen, W. (2015). Flexible work designs and employee well-being: Examining the effects of resources and demands. *New Technology, Work and Employment, 30*(3), 237–255. https://doi.org/10.1111/ntwe.12052.
39. Tremblay, M. S., Colley, R. C., Saunders, T. J., Healy, G. N., & Owen, N. (2010). Physiological and health implications of a sedentary lifestyle. *Applied Physiology, Nutrition and Metabolism, 35*(6), 725–740. https://doi.org/10.1139/h10-079.
40. Van Horn, J. E., Taris, T. W., Schaufeli, W. B., & Schreurs, P. J. (2004). The structure of occupational well-being: A study among Dutch teachers. *Journal of Occupational and Organizational Psychology, 77*(3), 365–375. https://doi.org/10.1348/0963179041752718.

CHAPTER 8

Physical Activity and Sedentary Behaviour in the Digital Workspace

Anthony Thompson

Abstract Insufficient physical activity is a significant threat to both employee and organisational health yet long bouts of uninterrupted sitting time and fewer opportunities for physical activity are hallmarks of many modern occupations. This chapter explores the challenges and opportunities faced by agile workers in maintaining healthy levels of physical activity during the workday. The barriers faced by organisations in supporting their agile workers to be physically active are also considered. Technology may serve as both a contributor and a potential solution to problem and the chapter will explore this idea alongside the business case for intervention.

Keywords Physical activity · Sedentary · Health · Exergame · Intervention · Workplace wellness

A. Thompson (✉)
Coventry University, Coventry, UK
e-mail: ab9738@coventry.ac.uk

8.1   INTRODUCTION

This chapter presents an overview of a crucial, but often overlooked, aspect of agile working; the importance of disrupting sedentary behaviour and maintaining regular physical activity during the working day. Insufficient physical activity and long bouts of uninterrupted sitting time are substantial health damaging behaviours which have far-reaching consequences for both the individual and their organisation. Whilst technology undoubtedly offers the potential for more flexible working practices, it also increases the potential for employees to put their physical health at risk. To date, many workplace health promotion interventions have aimed to address this issue but have predominantly considered the needs of employees with fixed work locations. Unsurprisingly, this can be of limited use to agile workers whose work locations can vary substantially. This chapter will therefore consider the unique challenges and opportunities faced by agile workers in protecting themselves from physical inactivity. The chapter will also explore the wider socio-economic impact of physical inactivity, the business case for intervention and technology-based solutions.

8.2   THE RISE OF PHYSICAL INACTIVITY: A PERFECT STORM FOR AGILE WORKERS

In the modern world, physical inactivity is a substantial threat to health and prosperity. At an individual level, physical activity increases the risk of developing certain cancers, heart disease, stroke and diabetes by 20–30% and can shorten the lifespan by 3–5 years [41]. Physical inactivity has also been linked to negative mental health outcomes such as depression [1] and anxiety [4]. Physical inactivity can also have a substantial economic burden. Within the European Union physical inactivity costs the economy approximately €80.4 billion per year, a figure which is expected to rise to €125 billion by 2030 [9]. Despite this, there has been a visible decline in employee physical activity levels over the past 50 years [7] with technology use being cited as a key driver of this change [10]. Notably, white-collar (knowledge) workers have become particularly vulnerable to sedentary behaviour, spending approximately two-thirds of the working day seated [34]. Counter-intuitively, flexible working practices can potentially compound this problem, with evidence suggesting that, in certain cases, work location flexibility can actually increase employee daily sitting time [29]. Despite increasing awareness of employee physical inactivity, the role that technology plays and the rise of flexible working practices, a shortage of literature exists that explores the impact on agile workers, a population directly affected by all of these factors.

8.3   CHALLENGES FOR AGILE WORKERS

Agile workers are an incredibly diverse population with substantial variance in: the number of hours spent remote working, the extent of interaction with colleagues, the types of technology used and the number and types of locations worked from [11]. Such diversity can make it difficult to implement interventions that address the specific needs of each agile worker. Agile workers also often mask symptoms of ill-health and are more accepting of poorer health outcomes than non-agile workers, because of their lower visibility to employers [38]. This can potentially lead to agile employees being 'out of sight, out of mind'. Connected to this, it has been suggested that agile workers may self-manage their health by using the flexibility of their work to incorporate more physical activity into the workday; for instance, by leveraging reduced commute times to attend health clubs [2]. However, schedule flexibility and location flexibility are poor predictors of physical activity in agile workers [16] and the percentage of employees categorised as a high health-risk, due to physical inactivity, is not significantly different between remote workers (38%) and non-remote workers (40.4%) [20].

Engaging with existing workplace health interventions may also be challenging for agile workers as barriers become more pronounced. Geographical distance from colleagues can make remote working a socially isolating experience [17]. Reduced social cues to limit unhealthy behaviours may contribute to agile workers adopting unhealthy behaviours such as reduced physical activity [20]. Remote e-workers also often work longer hours than those in fixed workplaces [18]. This can lead to a blurring of boundaries, which can limit the amount of time available for non-work activities [33], including time for exercise and the pursuit of health-related behaviours [41]. Furthermore, home offices tend to be less ergonomic than formal office environments and be less conducive to incidental physical activity [14]. Providing the same physical and ergonomic resources and equipment to individual agile workers may be costly and impractical. One way of compensating for this may be through leveraging technology.

8.4   TECHNOLOGY-ASSISTED
INTERVENTIONS FOR AGILE WORKERS

Many types of technology-assisted interventions have been developed to promote physical activity in employees including: computer prompts, wearable activity monitors (such as iWatches and pedometers), digital activity reminders via email, text messages, as well as websites which present users with information about physical activity interventions [37]. Whilst still in its early stages, meta-analytic evidence suggests that technology-assisted interventions are effective in increasing physical activity [8] and decreasing sedentary behaviour in workplace settings [37]. A key strength of technology-assisted interventions is that they are not bound to specific times or locations and can provide users with tailored information and feedback at an appropriate time and place [28]. They are, therefore, well suited to an increasingly agile workforce. Yet barriers may still remain, for instance, computer prompts can encourage physical activity yet may lack social interaction elements to make them engaging for agile workers. In the next section, an emerging tool—exergaming—will be considered as a potential solution for supporting physical activity in agile workers.

8.4.1   Exergaming

Exergaming is portmanteau of the words exercise and gaming [6] and has been defined as video games which have the potential to promote physical activity during screen time [22]. Whilst such games have traditionally been viewed as entertainment, research is increasingly seeing beneficial applications to health promotion within workplace settings [23, 30]. Exergames can help agile workers to overcome many of the barriers associated with location independent working. For instance, multi-player exergames allow two or more users to move, compete or exercise together regardless of their geographical distance [12]. Longer hours and non-traditional work schedules can also make it challenging for agile workers to coordinate their physical activity routines with colleagues, further compounding issues of social isolation. For those unable to 'play' at the same time as their colleagues, exergames such as TripleBeat [36] enable users to compete against each other asynchronously, comparing their performance against the past performance of others who have also played the game [27]. Such games offer agile workers the flexibility to engage with the same physical activity interventions as their colleagues, preserving the social element of the game, but at times which are most convenient for their working day.

From an organisational perspective, exergames can draw upon equipment that the agile worker is already likely to possess reducing the need for additional tools or devices, such as sit-stand desks. Exergames have been developed for use with smartphones and computer webcams. Smartphone exergames can draw upon geolocation, enabling users to customise their experience to their current location and also to share their route or location with other users nearby [25]. This can be particularly beneficial for agile workers who may move regularly between different, and sometimes unfamiliar, locations. Webcam-based exergames can allow users to access a library of exercises and mirror the actions performed onscreen with feedback [15]. Such exergames can also draw upon virtual, software-generated partners who can take on the role of either trainer or competitor [13]. This is advantageous from a health and safety perspective as virtual exergame instructors can help to facilitate correct technique and reduce the risk of injury, which is particularly important for agile workers who may be performing physical activity alone and unsupervised [39]. Meta-analytic investigations show strong promise for short bouts of exergames, demonstrating strong positive correlations between exergaming and energy expenditure at levels which meet physical activity guidelines for health and fitness [24]. Exergames have also been found to improve mental health and psychological well-being in users [40]; a factor particularly salient to agile workers.

8.5   THE BUSINESS CASE FOR PHYSICAL ACTIVITY

Employee ill-health has been estimated to cost British businesses approximately £81 billion per year, a figure comprising employee absence and reduced productivity through presenteeism [3]. Given that employers bear the financial burden of reduced productivity and sickness absence, organisations are increasingly turning to workplace wellness programmes as a method of disease prevention and cost reduction [21]. Workplace wellness programmes are organisationally endorsed interventions, which aim to encourage preventative care and discourage unhealthy behaviours [26] and have been shown to increase employee physical activity levels [31]. However, a key metric for any organisation considering the implementation of a new initiative is the return on investment.

Exact figures for the return on investment for workplace health promotion programmes can be mixed, ranging from small [35] through to large [9]. However, meta-analytic investigations have demonstrated a 30% return on investment for employers, with consistent reductions in the number of employee absence days [19]. Furthermore, participation in health promotion interventions has been demonstrated to increase employee productivity by approximately 10% [5] and significantly reduce voluntary employee turnover rates [32]. Given that the number of agile workers is anticipated to increase substantially by 2025 [32], organisations wishing to exploit the benefits of health promotions programmes will need to pay close attention to the needs of agile workers. Physical activity interventions are emerging as a cost-effective solution enabling organisations to simultaneously improve both employee physical and mental health.

8.6   CONCLUSION

Insufficient physical activity has far-reaching consequences for the health and productivity of both agile workers and their organisations. To date, physical activity interventions tailored specifically to the unique needs of agile workers remains limited and urgent research is needed. However, as this chapter has identified, whilst technology may be a key contributor to physical inactivity, it may also afford a variety of flexible solutions for agile workers in the digital age.

REFERENCES

1. Achttien, R., van Lieshout, J., Wensing, M., van der Sanden, M. N., & Staal, J. B. (2019). Symptoms of depression are associated with physical inactivity but not modified by gender or the presence of a cardiovascular disease, a cross-sectional study. *BMC Cardiovascular Disorders, 19*(1), 95. https://doi.org/10.1186/s12872-019-1065-8.
2. Allen, T. D., Golden, T. D., & Shockley, K. M. (2015). How effective is telecommuting? Assessing the status of our scientific findings. *Psychological Science in the Public Interest, 16*(2), 40–68. https://doi.org/10.1177/1529100615593273.
3. Baicker, K., Cutler, D., & Song, Z. (2010). Workplace wellness programs can generate savings. *Health Affairs, 29*(2), 304–311. https://doi.org/10.1377/hlthaff.2009.0626.

4. Bélair, M. A., Kohen, D. E., Kingsbury, M., & Colman, I. (2018). Relationship between leisure time physical activity, sedentary behaviour and symptoms of depression and anxiety: Evidence from a population-based sample of Canadian adolescents. *British Medical Journal Open, 8*(10), e021119. https://doi.org/10.1136/bmjopen-2017-021119.

5. Berry, L., Mirabito, A. M., & Baun, W. (2010, December). *What's the hard return on employee wellness programs? Harvard Business Review.* https://hbr.org/2010/12/whats-the-hard-return-on-employee-wellness-programs.

6. Best, J. R. (2013). Exergaming in youth: Effects on physical and cognitive health. *Zeitschrift Fur Psychologie, 221*(2), 72–78. https://doi.org/10.1027/2151-2604/a000137.

7. Brownson, R. C., Boehmer, T. K., & Luke, D. A. (2005). Declining rates of physical activity in the United States: What are the contributors? *Annual Review of Public Health, 26,* 421–443. https://doi.org/10.1146/annurev.publhealth.26.021304.144437.

8. Buckingham, S. A., Williams, A. J., Morrissey, K., Price, L., & Harrison, J. (2019). Mobile health interventions to promote physical activity and reduce sedentary behaviour in the workplace: A systematic review. *Digital Health, 5,* 2055207619839883. https://doi.org/10.1177/2055207619839883.

9. Centre for Economics and Business Research. (2015). *The Economic Cost of Physical Inactivity in Europe.* https://inactivity-time-bomb.nowwemove.com/download-report/The%20Economic%20Costs%20of%20Physical%20Inactivity%20in%20Europe%20(June%202015).pdf. Accessed 16 October 2019.

10. Church, T. S., Thomas, D. M., Tudor-Locke, C., Katzmarzyk, P. T., Earnest, C. P., Rodarte, R. Q., et al. (2011). Trends over 5 decades in U.S. occupation-related physical activity and their associations with obesity. *PLoS ONE, 6*(5), [e19657]. https://doi.org/10.1371/journal.pone.0019657.

11. Daniels, K., Lamond, D., & Standen, P. (2001). Teleworking: Frameworks for organizational research. *Journal of Management Studies, 38*(8), 1151–1185. https://doi.org/10.1111/1467-6486.00276.

12. De Oliveira, R., & Oliver, N. (2008). TripleBeat: Enhancing exercise performance with persuasion. In *Proceedings of the 10th International Conference on Human Computer Interaction with Mobile Devices and Services, Amsterdam, Netherlands* (pp. 255–264). https://doi.org/10.1145/1409240.1409268.

13. Doyle, J., Kelly, D., Patterson, M., & Caulfield, B. (2011). The effects of visual feedback in therapeutic exergaming on motor task accuracy. *Proceedings of International Conference on Virtual Rehabilitation, Zurich, Switzerland,* 1–5. https://doi.org/10.1109/ICVR.2011.5971821.

14. Edmunds, S., Hurst, L., & Harvey, K. (2013). Physical activity barriers in the workplace. *International Journal of Workplace Health Management*, 6(3), 227–240. https://doi.org/10.1108/IJWHM-11-2010-0040.

15. Feltz, D., & Samendinger, S. (2018). Exergames to enhance physical activity and performance. In T. Horn & A. Smith (Eds.), *Advances in sport and exercise psychology* (pp. 247–259). USA: Human Kinetics.

16. Goguen, K. (2017). *Flexible and fit: Examining the relationship between flexible work arrangements and employee health*. Unpublished doctoral dissertation, Clemson University. https://tigerprints.clemson.edu/cgi/viewcontent.cgi?article=2978&context=all_dissertations. Accessed 14 January 2020.

17. Golden, T. D., Veiga, J. F., & Dino, R. N. (2008). The impact of professional isolation on teleworker job performance and turnover intentions: Does time spent teleworking, interacting face-to-face, or having access to communication-enhancing technology matter? *Journal of Applied Psychology*, 93(6), 1412–1421. https://doi.org/10.1037/a0012722.

18. Grant, C. A., Wallace, L. M., & Spurgeon, P. C. (2013). An exploration of the psychological factors affecting remote e-worker's job effectiveness, well-being and work-life balance. *Employee Relations.*, 35(5), 527–546. https://doi.org/10.1108/ER-08-2012-0059.

19. Gubler, T., Larkin, I., & Pierce, L. (2018). Doing well by making well: The impact of corporate wellness programs on employee productivity. *Management Science*, 64(11), 4967–4987. https://doi.org/10.1287/mnsc.2017.2883.

20. Henke, R. M., Benevent, R., Schulte, P., Rinehart, C., Crighton, K. A., & Corcoran, M. (2016). The effects of telecommuting intensity on employee health. *American Journal of Health Promotion*, 30(8), 604–612. https://doi.org/10.4278/ajhp.141027-quan-544.

21. Jones, D., Molitor, D., & Reif, J. (2019). What do workplace wellness programs do? Evidence from the Illinois workplace wellness study. *The Quarterly Journal of Economics*, 134(4), 1747–1791. https://doi.org/10.3386/w24229.

22. Lanningham-Foster, L., Jensen, T. B., Foster, R. C., Redmond, A. B., Walker, B. A., Heinz, D., et al. (2006). Energy expenditure of sedentary screen time compared with active screen time for children. *Paediatrics*, 118(6), 1831–1835. https://doi.org/10.1123/pes.19.3.334.

23. Li, J., Theng, Y. L., Cheong, W. L., Hoo, Y. F., & Ngo, M. D. (2016). Exergames for the corporate wellness program in Singapore: An investigation of employees' acceptance via watching Kinect video. *Digital Health*, 2, 1–8. https://doi.org/10.1177/2055207616654578.

24. Li, J., Theng, Y. L., & Foo, S. (2016). Effect of exergames on depression: A systematic review and meta-analysis. *Cyberpsychology, Behavior, and Social Networking*, 19(1), 34–42. https://doi.org/10.1089/cyber.2015.0366.

25. Losilla, F., & Rosique, F. (2019). An augmented reality mirror exergame using 2d pose estimation. In *Proceedings of the 14th International Conference on Software Technologies, ICSOFT, Prague, Czech Republic, 1,* 643–648. https://doi.org/10.5220/0007798906430648.
26. Lowensteyn, I., Berberian, V., Belisle, P., DaCosta, D., Joseph, L., & Grover, S. A. (2018). The measurable benefits of a workplace wellness program in Canada. *Journal of Occupational and Environmental Medicine, 60*(3), 211–216. https://doi.org/10.1097/JOM.0000000000001240.
27. Marins, D. R., de OD Justo, M., Xexeo, G. B., de AM Chaves, B., & D'Ipolitto, C. (2011, November). SmartRabbit: A mobile exergame using geolocation. In *Proceedings of the 2011 Brazilian Symposium on Games and Digital Entertainment, Salvador, Brazil* (pp. 232–240). https://doi.org/10.1109/SBGAMES.2011.34.
28. Middelweerd, A., Mollee, J. S., van der Wal, C. N., Brug, J., & Te Velde, S. J. (2014). Apps to promote physical activity among adults: A review and content analysis. *International Journal of Behavioral Nutrition and Physical Activity, 11*(1), 97. https://doi.org/10.1186/s12966-014-0097-9.
29. Olsen, H., Brown, W., Kolbe-Alexander, T., & Burton, N. (2018). Flexible work—The impact of a new policy on employees' sedentary behavior and physical activity. *Journal of Occupational and Environmental Medicine, 60*(1), 23–28. https://doi.org/10.1097/JOM.0000000000001190.
30. Park, T., Hwang, I., Lee, U., Lee, S.I., Yoo, C., Lee, Y., et al. (2012). ExerLink: Enabling pervasive social exergames with heterogeneous exercise devices. In *Proceedings of the 10th international conference on Mobile systems, applications, and services, Lake District, UK* (pp. 15–28). https://doi.org/10.1145/2307636.2307639.
31. RAND. (2014). *Do workplace wellness programs save employers money?* https://www.rand.org/content/dam/rand/pubs/research_briefs/RB9700/RB9744/RAND_RB9744.pdf. Accessed 14 January 2020.
32. Randstad. (2017). *Workplace 2025.* https://www.randstadusa.com/workforce360/2017-workplace-2025/. Accessed 20 February 2020.
33. Robertson, M. M., Maynard, W. S., & McDevitt, J. R. (2003). Telecommuting: Managing the safety of workers in home office environments. *Professional Safety, 48*(4), 30–36.
34. Ryde, G. C., Brown, H. E., Gilson, N. D., & Brown, W. J. (2014). Are we chained to our desks? Describing desk-based sitting using a novel measure of occupational sitting. *Journal of Physical Activity and Health, 11*(7), 1318–1323. https://doi.org/10.1123/jpah.2012-0480.
35. Schaefer, J. (2015, February 24). *The real ROI for employee wellness programs.* SHRM. https://www.shrm.org/resourcesandtools/hr-topics/benefits/pages/real-roi-wellness.aspx. Accessed 14 January 2020.

36. Stach, T. (2010). *Design aspects of multiplayer exergames* (Technical Report 2010-571). Queen's University, Canada. https://research.cs.queensu.ca/TechReports/Reports/2010-571.pdf.
37. Stephenson, A., McDonough, S. M., Murphy, M. H., Nugent, C. D., & Mair, J. L. (2017). Using computer, mobile and wearable technology enhanced interventions to reduce sedentary behaviour: A systematic review and meta-analysis. *International Journal of Behavioral Nutrition and Physical Activity, 14*(1), 105. https://doi.org/10.1186/s12966-017-0561-4.
38. Steward, B. (2000). Fit to telework-The changing meaning of fitness in new forms of employment. *Advances in Physiotherapy, 2*(3), 103–111. https://doi.org/10.1080/14038190050175781.
39. Sween, J., Wallington, S., Sheppard, V., Taylor, T., Llanos, A. A., & Adams-Campbell, L. (2014). The role of exergaming in improving physical activity: A review. *Journal of Physical Activity and Health, 11*(4), 864–870.
40. Vitality. (2019). *British businesses could save £61 billion per year by prioritising health and well-being.* https://www.vitality.co.uk/media/british-businesses-could-save-61-billion-pounds-per-year-prioritising-health-well-being/. Accessed 14 January 2020.
41. World Health Organization. (n.d.). *Physical Activity.* https://www.who.int/health-topics/physical-activity#tab=tab_1. Accessed 12 February 2020.

CHAPTER 9

Digital Resilience: A Competency Framework for Agile Workers

Christine Grant and Carl Clarke

Abstract This chapter presents the latest research on how to effectively support agile workers, their managers and organisations build digital resilience using a competency-based approach. Organisations need to support and develop competencies for agile workers for the twenty-first century, and yet this is an area largely overlooked in the literature. The development of a digital resilience framework outlines the core competencies for sustainable agile working, grounded in emerging research. The chapter concludes by outlining how organisations can apply this digital resilience framework to support agile working practices.

C. Grant
School of Psychological, Social and Behavioural Sciences,
Coventry University, Coventry, UK
e-mail: christine.grant@coventry.ac.uk

C. Clarke (✉)
FCIPD, London, UK

Keywords Competencies · Competency · Knowledge, skills, attitudes and behaviours · Self-determination theory · Conservation of resource theory · Agile working · Remote e-working · E-working · Resilience · Digital

9.1   INTRODUCTION

The pace of technological change in the last decade has been profound, a trend set to accelerate following the 2019/2020 Coronavirus pandemic (COVID-19). The development and adoption of new digital tools and digitally mediated communications has changed the way in which people work, access, consume and communicate information, developments key to agile working. These advancements have provided significant benefits to employers and employees, while also escalating the development of constantly connected work cultures [11]. Studies show that when workers forego the emotional, mental and physical restorative effects of 'switching off', they are likely to experience a deterioration of work-life balance, well-being, job effectiveness and performance [4]. Moreover, with employers having a legal duty of care to protect worker health and safety, a deterioration in well-being potentially increases risks associated with work-based injuries and ill health, contributing to lost productivity, lower levels of engagement and financial, human and reputational damage.

The question facing employers and employees is how to embrace the benefits that new technologies bring to agile working, while mitigating their negative effects. Recent studies have explored the competencies needed to counteract the negative effects of digital-stressors at work [6, 7, 9]. These studies advocate that—by developing specific competencies—workers are better placed to mitigate digital-stressors and in turn are more able to incorporate technology into everyday life in a sustainable and healthy way [6].

9.2   DEFINING COMPETENCY FRAMEWORKS AND THEIR ADOPTION WITHIN ORGANISATIONS

Competency frameworks (CFs) have been used across a variety of sectors to assess job roles for many years [2, 8]. Competency-based approaches to predicting human performance differ from trait or intelligence-based approaches and are underpinned by two key assumptions: first, competencies can be observed, and second, competencies can be learned [1]. We define a 'competency' as the knowledge, skills, attitudes and behaviours that an individual, team or organisation needs to acquire to perform a current or future task well [1]. Within this definition: 'knowledge' is the assimilation of information through learning; 'skills' is the ability to apply knowledge to complete tasks and solve problems; 'attitudes' are the feelings, values and beliefs a person holds, which influence the performance of a task; 'behaviour' is observable conduct towards others [13, 15].

Adopting a competency-based approach has a range of benefits [5]. Clearly defined competencies clarify what is required to be successful and supports individual and organisational alignment on performance expectations. CFs can underpin recruitment and appraisal processes and provide a fair approach to assessing performance. Frameworks standardise assessment processes across organisations, which is particularly relevant when similar roles are being performed in different geographic locations. Finally, CFs can support the translation of values into expected employee behaviours, aiding alignment between organisational goals and culture. Despite these benefits, organisations typically face development, implementation and sustainability challenges when adopting competency-based practices. CFs can fail to evolve fast enough to reflect the emergence of new competencies, quickly reducing their overall effectiveness. While there is debate on the relevance and application of CFs, having a clearly defined set of competencies does set expectations on what is required for high performance within organisations/job roles, and for this reason they are considered a useful tool. However, to provide ongoing meaning, CFs need to be refreshed to reflect organisational and technological change, with new competencies quickly codified to ensure competitive advantage is secured.

Agile workers have a unique set of requirements for delivering effective performance. Agile working can involve negotiating work-home boundaries, responding rapidly to customer and client needs, managing digital technologies and being innovative [10]. In this chapter, we consider the issue of e-working as an agile working practice and the adoption and effective use of digital technologies to facilitate this type of working. The next section discusses a new concept of 'digital resilience' and how this may be supported and promoted by developing and implementing a CF for e-workers.

9.3 Defining Digital Resilience

Employers need to find ways to integrate technology into the employee experience so that e-working benefits are realised, and digital-stressors are mitigated [6]. The term 'digital-stressors' refers to any negative effects that technology may have on the user [23]. This is an umbrella term, recognising that there is no common definition of digital stress (also known as technostress: stress caused by technology), with technophobia, cyberphobia, computerphobia, anxiety and computer stress all cited as examples in the literature [22]. Tarafdar et al. [20] provide a framework to understand how technology-use contributes to stress, citing five reasons: technology overload, invasion, complexity, insecurity and uncertainty [20].

'Resilience' is defined as a process to 'negotiate, adapt and manage stresses' enabling individuals to 'bounce back' in the face of adversity [24, p. 2]. Our focus is on how to support e-workers as they negotiate, adapt and manage the stressors that arise from the incorporation of technology into everyday life. The Conservation of Resources (COR) theory provides a useful framework to explore this. COR theory is underpinned by a belief that individuals are motivated to acquire, build and protect resources in order to achieve their goals; stress occurs when (a) resources are lost or threatened and (b) there is a failure to gain resources following significant effort [12, p. 104]. Two distinct types of resources are identified: contextual and personal [3]. Contextual resources are located outside the individual and set in the broader environment. These resources include social support, autonomy and opportunities for development and feedback, whereas personal resources are inherent to the individual and include physical, psychological, affective, intellectual and capital resources [3]. Knowledge, skills, attitudes and behaviours (i.e. competencies) are considered to be personal resources that can be developed over time. The more resources an individual has, the more effective they are at responding to situations. Resources can also be mutually reinforcing, with increases in one area generating resources in another. Hobfoll et al. [12] describe this as 'resource caravans', indicating that resources do not exist individually, but travel in packs [12]. For instance, job autonomy (contextual resource) is likely to increase when e-workers work remotely. In turn this may lead to a reduced commute, with time saved (personal resource) enabling more time to be spent with the family (contextual resource). In this instance, the acquisition of contextual and personal resources creates a buffer against digital-stressors (i.e. longer working hours, social isolation).

Building resources is, therefore, a way to build resilience, enabling individuals to negotiate, adapt to and manage stressors. A limited number of studies consider whether resilience per se is a resource that can be developed, with emerging studies confirming the importance of knowledge building (personal resource) and the value of social networks, social support and relationships (contextual resources) [16, 17]. Studies in this area are limited, with research typically centred on children, students and high-risk groups. The term digital resilience refers to the specific knowledge, skills, attitudes and behaviours (personal resources or competencies) that need to be acquired, built and protected to counteract the negative effects of digital-stressors [7]. Through building digital resilience, e-workers would be better placed to negotiate, adapt and manage the negative psychological effects of digital-stressors, in turn, improving well-being and workplace outcomes. Building digital resilience is a two-way process occurring at an individual and organisational level [6]. Organisations are responsible for ensuring that work and organisational structures are designed to reduce unnecessary stressors being imposed on workers. Individuals are responsible for utilising resources that are available to them to optimise their well-being [6].

9.4   COMPETENCIES REQUIRED FOR E-WORKING

Three research studies have enabled the development of an emerging CF for digital resilience. In study one, a qualitative study of 34 exemplary remote e-workers provided and confirmed a list of 21 e-worker competencies focusing on job effectiveness, work-life balance and well-being (Table 9.1) [9]. In study two, the 21 competencies were reviewed and categorised according to self-determination theory, providing a theoretical framework to consider how e-workers are motivated (Table 9.2) [7]. In study three, a mixed methods study of 345 e-workers completed a survey to assess their e-working digital resilience and to confirm the 21 competencies [6]. This was followed by 11 semi-structured interviews to establish themes to support the framework and categorise the competencies. The three studies confirm the original 21 competencies and identify five over-arching themes that could be used as categories to devise a CF for digital resilience. Further details on the studies can be found in the references.

9.4.1   Supporting Theory

Self-determination theory (SDT) considers how psychological needs can best be supported to enable workers' personal growth, well-being and

Table 9.1   E-worker competencies identified in study one [9]

Competency	Definition
Self-management and discipline	Managing self to ensure work objectives and goals are met, when working from multiple locations
Autonomy	Being able to manage own work to ensure tasks are delivered on time and to desired quality, irrespective of where and when work is delivered
Time management skills	Able to manage work and non-work time to complete objectives, being aware of and setting boundaries to manage work and non-working hours effectively
Self-motivation	Able to deliver work objectives and outputs without supervision and from any location
Prioritisation skills	Able to prioritise important deadlines over non-urgent tasks to deliver outputs, self-managing time
Organisational skills	Able to organise work effectively to achieve work goals, irrespective of location
Integrity	Able to think through and make timely decisions, deferring for support only when needed and, considers all options effectively
Developing trust	Develops and inspires trust with manager, peers and reportees, even when physical engagement is limited
Manages social relationships through technology	Able to use technology to develop diverse relationships and build peer support to achieve work goals and facilitate team engagement, irrespective of work location
Adaptability	Uses technology as an enabler to adapt to changes in workload and pressures, ensuring that peers and reportees are supported
Self-care of health/health awareness	Understands how technology impacts own and others well-being, considers health needs, acts when feeling unwell and/or where support is needed from others
Emotional self-efficacy	Able to effectively manage negative moods which may occur when working alone, ensures support is sought if required
Communication skills	Apt at choosing the best communication method for the task and uses different technologies to build rapport with others effectively
Tenacity	Overcomes setbacks to complete tasks, establishes a network to ensure effective ways are found to complete difficult goals
Self-confidence	Able to support oneself when working remotely, confident to take decisions based on evidence
Coping styles	Aware of and deploys different coping strategies to support agile working, while protecting own health

(continued)

Table 9.1   (continued)

Competency	Definition
Self-awareness	Understands when over-working, able to switch off from work/technology as appropriate
Social support	Develops and maintains a diverse network of colleagues, friends and family to turn to for support when working remotely
Cognitive flexibility	Finds imaginative solutions to work problems utilising new technology and remote networks
Networking	Develops a diverse and effective work and social network that supports work and non-work activities and uses technology to facilitate communication
I.T. knowledge and skills	Continuously builds knowledge and know-how on technology and its use in supporting agile working

Table 9.2   E-working competencies mapped to self-determination theory [7]

	Competence	Autonomy	Relatedness
Attitudes and behaviours	Integrity Adaptability Tenacity Self-confidence Cognitive flexibility Emotional self-efficacy	Self-management and discipline Autonomy Self-motivation	Self-awareness Developing trust
Skills	Organisational skills	Time management skills Prioritisation skills	Communication skills Manages social relationships through technology Social support networking
Knowledge	Coping styles I.T. knowledge and skills	Self-care of health/health awareness	

effectiveness. As such, it provides a useful backdrop to the development of the digital resilience framework. SDT advocates that people are inherently proactive and have a tendency towards growth and integrated functioning; these are key facets as workers seek to integrate technology into their working lives [19]. SDT argues that only when three basic psychological needs are met will growth and functioning be enjoyed.

These needs are: competence (sense of effectiveness, mastery), autonomy (control and choice within one's environment) and relatedness (connectedness, sense of belonging) [21]. The extent to which these needs are met directly and indirectly affects well-being and workplace outcomes [14, 18]. Therefore, through the process of building e-worker competence, e-workers begin to acquire the resources (digital resilience) to fulfil these three basic needs. This enables e-workers to self-regulate and integrate technology into their working lives in a healthy and sustainable way. Table 9.2 shows e-worker competencies identified in study one mapped to the SDT framework compiled in study two.

9.5   Digital Resilience Competency Framework

Study three expanded on study one and two and identified five overachieving themes [6] that could be used to build a digital resilience framework for e-workers. The themes clustered together the 21 competencies identified in study one and two and are:

   i. Social and relational
  ii. Trust
 iii. Knowledge
  iv. Personal efficiency
   v. Self-care.

The five themes will now be explored, supported by additional study three findings, further refining the framework (see Table 9.3).

9.5.1   Social and Relational Competencies

Correlation with other measures, including technostress, revealed a positive relationship between low social and relational competencies and high technostress. This confirms the importance that social competencies (social competence, social resources, family cohesion) have on mitigating stressors and supports the competencies: managing social relationships through technology, networking, communication skills and social support and largely supports resource building to satisfy relatedness needs in SDT.

Table 9.3 Digital resilience competency framework to support e-workers

Themes (link to SDT in brackets)	Competencies
Social and relational competencies (*Relatedness*)	• Managing social skills through technology • Networking • Social support • Communication skills
Trust (*Autonomy, relatedness and competence*)	• Developing trust • Organisational skills • Autonomy • Integrity
Knowledge (*Competence needs*)	• I.T. knowledge and skills • Adaptability • Tenacity • Self-confidence
Personal efficiency (*Autonomy and relatedness*)	• Self-management and discipline • Self-motivation • Prioritisation skills • Time management skills • Self-awareness • Cognitive flexibility
Self-care (*Autonomy and relatedness*)	• Emotional self-efficacy • Self-care of health/health awareness • Coping styles

9.5.2   Trust

Trusting team members to deliver work and avoiding micro-management was found to be an important facet of delivering effective e-working. Trust is multi-directional and needs to be developed over time and jointly to support mutual respect. The importance of the manager in developing a trusting relationship is not surprising and frequently appears as a topic in management, well-being and motivational theory. However, the complexity of e-working may require the trust-related competencies to evolve to reflect a new employment context where employees can work anywhere and anytime [6]. These findings are supportive of the competencies: developing trust, organisational skills, autonomy, prioritisation skills, and integrity and appear to support resource building to satisfy competence, autonomy and relatedness in SDT.

9.5.3   Knowledge of Tools and Technology to Support E-Working

Participants recognised that technology and its effective use was key to enabling successful e-working. The challenge raised by participants was a lack of understanding on what and how tools should be used. For instance, participants wondered when to use email versus online collaboration tools or when and how to use video conferencing to support and facilitate team engagement. This led to participant frustration, with communications being duplicated or missed. Increasing literacy on digital tools combined with broadening understanding on how and when to use tools would aid user effectiveness and decrease stress caused by lack of clarity and knowledge. These findings are supportive of the competencies: emotional self-efficacy, adaptability, tenacity, self-confidence and I.T. knowledge and skills, with all elements supporting competence resource building in SDT. Chapter 10 examines the management of virtual teams in more depth.

9.5.4   Personal Efficiency

A positive relationship between low personal efficiency and high technostress was found. This suggests that by building efficiency competencies workers would be better placed to mitigate stressors caused by e-working, that is, more able to manage longer, more intense hours and the blurring of work-home (non-work) boundaries, factors cited as negative consequences of e-working and a drain on resources. These findings are supportive of the competencies: self-management and discipline, self-motivation, time management skills, self-awareness, communications skills and cognitive flexibility and likely support the building of resources to fulfil autonomy and relatedness needs in SDT.

9.5.5   Self-Care

In study three, around 20% of survey participants indicated that they did not know when they needed to switch off from technology and more than 15% of participants did not know what action to take when being constantly connected became too much [6]. This suggests that some workers may already be experiencing the negative effects of constant connectivity without fully understanding the impact it may be having on their well-being. This reconfirms the importance of self-care of health/health awareness, self-awareness and coping styles competencies and the importance of satisfying autonomy and relatedness SDT needs.

9.6 PRACTICAL WAYS TO BUILD DIGITAL RESILIENCE AND UTILISE THE NEW COMPETENCY FRAMEWORK

The exploratory findings allow us to provide practical guidance to organisations, managers and e-workers on the competencies that need to be developed to support digital resilience. For roles that require e-working, assessing digital resilience competencies would provide an indication of how successful somone might be in managing agile working and where specific competencies needed to be developed and supported [6]. Assessments could take place prior to employees starting a period of e-working, enabling appropriate interventions to be put in place from the outset.

Within the digital resilience framework, organisations can support the development of e-worker **knowledge and personal efficiency** competencies. For instance, building knowledge on specific I.T. products and tools could increase user understanding, acceptance and efficacy. Targeted skill building programmes could also be run, for instance on time management and prioritisation, or how to communicate effectively through different digital channels. Organisations could also establish programmes to develop **manager competence** in leading virtual and remote teams. This recognises that the context in which a manager executes their role has changed, impacting how trust is built, relationships are developed and engagement is sustained within teams.

Establishing a team charter for e-workers would support the development of **social and relational competencies**. Charters could provide guidance on when and how teams should utilise technology to support team engagement, how frequently teams should connect and through which media. This would reduce e-worker confusion, ensure desired behaviours are understood and facilitate the development of supportive relationships. This could be reinforced by socio-mapping techniques, whereby the strength of relationships within and across teams is periodically reviewed and interventions made to increase connections. This seeks to overcome concerns over social isolation and ensures team relationships continually evolve, despite individuals potentially being dispersed.

It would also ensure new joiners clearly understood expectations of how to work within a team, which could be further reinforced through virtual buddies or team coaches.

Finally, to develop **self-care competencies**, organisations can increase awareness of the risks and mitigators of e-working. Individuals can also develop their own awareness skills to better recognise the signs of when agile working may no longer be working for the individual and whether a different response is required.

9.7   Conclusion

This research provides the developmental stages of an original and previously unpublished competency framework for managing digital resilience. This framework is linked to two theoretical models: COR theory, which highlights the need to build resources to offset digital-stressors, and SDT, which indicates how resources might be directed to satisfy three key psychological needs. The framework has postulated five over-arching themes that can be used as categories to organise the competencies and help direct organisations towards developing particular themes to better support and develop e-worker digital resilience. This framework can now be utilised by e-workers, managers and organisations to support agile working, with a focus on improving well-being. This not only benefits e-workers in terms of building digital resilience but also has the potential to improve work-based outcomes and help organisations to meet their legal obligations and protect against potential human, financial and reputational damages.

References

1. Athey, T. R., & Orth, M. S. (1999). Emerging competency methods for the future. *Human Resource Management, 38*(3), 215–225. https://doi.org/10.1002/(SICI)1099-050X(199923)38:3%3c215:AID-HRM4%3e3.0.CO;2-W.

2. Boyatzis, R. (2008). Competencies in the 21st century. *Journal of Management Development, 27*(1), 5–12. https://doi.org/10.1108/02621710810810840730.

3. ten Brummelhuis, L. L., & Bakker, A. (2012). A resource perspective on the work-home interface: The work-home resources model. *American Psychologist, 67*(7), 545–556. https://doi.org/10.1037/a0027974.

4. Charalampous, M., Grant, C. A., Tramontano, C., & Michailidis, E. (2019). Systematically reviewing remote e-workers' well-being at work: A multidimensional approach. *European Journal of Work and Organizational Psychology, 28*(1), 51–73. https://doi.org/10.1080/1359432X.2018.154 1886.

5. CIPD. (2020). *Competence and competency frameworks* [Fact sheet]. https://www.cipd.co.uk/knowledge/fundamentals/people/performance/competency-factsheet. Accessed 3 May 2020.

6. Clarke, C. (2018). *An exploratory study to examine the knowledge, skills, abilities, and behaviours needed to build digital resilience in an 'always on' culture within a large telecommunications organisation* (Unpublished M.Sc. dissertation, Ed.). Coventry University.

7. Clarke, C., Grant, C. A., & Russell, E. (2019, May 29–June 1). A study into the knowledge, skills, abilities, and behaviours needed in an 'always on' workplace [Conference Presentation]. In *19th Congress of the European Association of Work and Organizational Psychology (EAWOP)*, Turin, Italy (Unpublished).

8. Le Deist, F. D., & Winterton, J. (2005). What is competence? *Human Resource Development International, 8*(1), 27–46. https://doi.org/10.1080/1367886042000338227.

9. Grant, C. A., & Kinman, G. (2017, May 17–20). E-worker resilience: A competency-based approach to ameliorate the impact of technology on well-being [Conference Presentation]. In *European Academy of Work and Organisational Psychology Conference*, Dublin, Ireland (Published).

10. Grant, C. A., & Russell, E. (2020). *Agile working and well-being in the digital age.* London: Palgrave Macmillan.

11. Grant, C. A., Wallace, L., & Spurgeon, P. (2013). An exploration of the psychological factors affecting remote e-worker's job effectiveness, well-being, and work-life balance. *Employee Relations, 35*(5), 527–546. https://doi.org/10.1108/ER-08-2012-0059.

12. Hobfoll, S., Halbesleben, J., Neveu, J.-P., & Westman, M. (2018). Conservation of resources in the organizational context: The reality of resources and their consequences. *Annual Review of Organizational Psychology and Organizational Behaviour, 5*(1), 103–128. https://doi.org/10.1146/annurev-orgpsych-032117-104640.

13. Kirinic, V., & Kozina, M. (2018). Analysis of quality-related competencies within the European e-Competence Framework (e-CF). In *2018 4th International Conference on Information Management, (ICIM) Proceedings* (pp. 170–174). Oxford, UK. https://doi.org/10.1109/INFOMAN.2018.8392829.

14. Maryle, M., Gagné, M., & Deci, E. (2005). Self-determination theory and work motivation. *Journal of Organizational Behaviour, 26*(4), 331–362. https://doi.org/10.1002/job.322.
15. Mills, J. A., Middleton, J., Schafer, A., Fitzpatrick, S., Short, S., & Cieza, A. (2020). Proposing a re-conceptualisation of competency framework terminology for health: A scoping review. *Human Resources for Health, 18*(1), 1–16. https://doi.org/10.1186/s12960-019-0443-8.
16. Nakashima, M., & Canda, E. (2005). Positive dying and resiliency in later life: A qualitative study. *Journal of Aging Studies, 19*(1), 109–125. https://doi.org/10.1016/j.jaging.2004.02.002.
17. O'Dwyer, S., Moyle, W., & van Wyk, S. (2013). Suicidal ideation and resilience in family carers of people with dementia: A pilot qualitative study. *Aging and Mental Health, 17*(6), 753–760. https://doi.org/10.1080/136 07863.2013.789001.
18. Reis, H., Sheldon, K., Gable, S., Roscoe, J., & Ryan, R. (2000). Daily well-being: The role of autonomy, competence, and relatedness. *Personality and Social Psychology Bulletin, 26*(4), 419–435. https://doi.org/10.1177/014 6167200266002.
19. Ryan, R., & Deci, E. (2000). Self-determination theory and the facilitation of intrinsic motivation, social development, and well-being. *American Psychologist, 55*(1), 68–78. https://doi.org/10.1037110003-066X.55.1.68.
20. Tarafdar, M., Tu, Q., Ragu-Nathan, B. S., & Ragu-Nathan, T. S. (2007). The impact of technostress on role stress and productivity. *Journal of Management Information Systems, 24*(1), 301–328. https://doi.org/10. 2753/MIS0742-1222240109.
21. Vansteenkiste, M., & Ryan, R. (2013). On psychological growth and vulnerability: Basic psychological need satisfaction and need frustration as a unifying principle. *Journal of Psychotherapy Integration, 23*(3), 263–280. https://doi.org/10.1037/A0032359.
22. Wang, K., Shu, Q., & Tu, Q. (2008). Technostress under different organizational environments: An empirical investigation. *Computers in Human Behaviour, 24*(6), 3002–3013. https://doi.org/10.1016/j.chb. 2008.05.007.
23. Weil, M., & Rosen, L. (1997). *TechnoStress: Coping with technology @work @home @play*. New York: Wiley.
24. Windle, G., Bennett, K., & Noyes, J. (2011). A methodological review of resilience measurement scales. *Health and Quality of Life Outcomes, 9*(1), 1–18. https://doi.org/10.1186/1477-7525-9-8.

PART V

Dynamic and Innovative Approaches to Managing Agile Working

CHAPTER 10

Virtual Teams as Creative and Agile Work Environments

Petros Chamakiotis

Abstract Virtual teams are a dominant form of agile work; on the one hand, offering unparalleled benefits, while at the same time raising challenges for leaders and members in terms of successful delivery of their projects. This chapter discusses how virtual teams can best be managed, drawing on extant literature, with a focus on ensuring that employees' well-being is not sacrificed in the name of project success. Further to synthesising key literature in this area, the chapter presents current trends and directions for future research in the virtual team literature, as well as actionable items for those directly involved in virtual teamwork.

Keywords Virtual teams · Management · Connectivity · Creativity · Well-being

P. Chamakiotis (✉)
ESCP Business School, Madrid, Spain
e-mail: pchamakiotis@escp.eu

C. Grant and E. Russell (eds.), *Agile Working and Well-Being in the Digital Age*, https://doi.org/10.1007/978-3-030-60283-3_10

133

10.1   INTRODUCTION

The increasing adoption of digital technologies to afford more agile working has given rise to flexible and virtual work arrangements that offer possibilities for 24/7 productivity, higher agility, team member well-being, creativity and innovation [10]. As a result, many projects nowadays take place in virtual (project) team (VT) environments [30]. A VT is broadly defined as a group of dispersed individuals who collaborate virtually in order to accomplish (a) project (or organisational) goal(s) [14]. VTs constitute a unique form of agile working and differ from traditional teams, primarily due to: (a) the technology-mediated character of their members' communications [11]; (b) their high degree, and different types, of dispersion (e.g. geographical, temporal) [17]; and (c) the ensuing discontinuities of geography and culture, among others, which may disrupt team cohesion and performance [29].

VTs are enabled by, and dependent on, digital technologies which have advanced insofar that we are now reimagining where and when we work and the amount of agency we can exert over these possibilities. Kolb [15] introduced the concept of connectivity (from a socio-technical perspective) to describe the enabling potential of digital technologies for individuals to work in non-traditional environments, including beyond regular working hours and places (e.g. from home, cafés or while travelling/commuting). These connectivity-enabled possibilities offer more autonomy and flexibility and have been considered ideal environments for creativity and innovation [7]. Paradoxically, however, they may also have negative implications for individuals' sense of well-being and work-life balance [20]. Despite these developments, the VT literature has not looked at how ubiquitous connectivity might influence the management of work and the sense of well-being of VT members.

Over the years, scholars have examined some of the challenges associated with VTs, generally concluding that effective management is paramount to VT success. This chapter is aimed to inform practitioners who either work or are expected to transition into a VT environment, along with scholars in the field of agile working. The chapter starts with a discussion of the unique characteristics of VTs and the idiosyncrasies of their management and social exchanges within the VT context. Presented next are the current trends and fertile areas of research in the VT literature, followed by a section on actionable items for VT managers and members. With the recent COVID-19 pandemic forcing organisations to 'go virtual' [2], such a focus has become more opportune than ever.

10.2 MANAGEMENT AND UNIQUE
CHARACTERISTICS OF VTs

Early VT literature grew out of fields within the information systems (IS) community that focused on such concepts as computer-supported cooperative work (CSCW) [26] and computer-mediated communication (CMC) [28]. These fields highlighted the boundaryless and dispersed (or distributed) aspects of virtual teamwork that render it different from traditional, physically collocated ways of working. VTs are distinct because of the technology-mediated nature of their members' interactions, and the three different types of dispersion characterising them. Geographical/spatial dispersion refers to VTs where members are based in different locations (varying from as narrow as different floors in the same building through to different countries and continents). Temporal dispersion refers to dispersed members working together in a 'round-the-clock' fashion (often as a result of global geographical dispersion). Organisational dispersion describes individuals who may be affiliated to different parent organisations, who have joined a VT for the purposes of a specific project [19].

Different forms of dispersion can introduce discontinuities [29], and by extension, management challenges, including managing highly heterogenous teams [27], dealing with intra-team subgroup dynamics [23] and managing members' well-being [1]. There is consensus among scholars that suitable management practices, and attention to specific factors, are necessary in order to overcome those challenges. For example, coordination practices may vary from *tight* (involving frequent communications with virtual teammates, thus reducing uncertainty owed to VT discontinuities) to *loose* (with less frequent meetings but more actual collaboration) during the early stages of the innovation process [5]. Similarly, the extant VT literature has shed light on the factors influencing the expression of creativity within this context. For instance, creativity enhancers (e.g. stimulating colleagues) and inhibitors (e.g. technical issues) have been identified [22], while Chamakiotis et al. [7] identify individual (e.g. organisational skills), team (e.g. subgroups) and technology-related (e.g. (a)synchronicity) factors with an either enhancing or an inhibiting role, depending on the situation. Creativity is also best managed following a shared or emergent leadership style. These styles are more customary in VTs because of the flat hierarchies and the greater degrees of responsibility and autonomy that characterise them [4, 8].

When aiming for creative outputs, different leadership styles might coexist during the VT lifecycle with experts in different areas of work assuming responsibility for different types of task either successively (i.e. at different stages of the lifecycle) or simultaneously (i.e. a form of co-leadership found when two individuals lead different facets of the project within the same stage) [6]. To illustrate this, one research participant explains how mechanical engineers and industrial designers spearheaded different facets of a project:

> As mechanical guys, we took care of the prototype building work, working on moulds, electrical components and basically making a prototype we had decided to work on. The designers mainly worked on the stall, the poster and publicity material/posters/leaflets to exhibit on the final day [...] they took responsibility for all the design. [6, p. 38]

Specific actions that enable VT leaders to foster engagement (as a process that takes place as a project evolves) involve: (a) developing engagement (e.g. providing clarity about pay conditions, team introductions); (b) supporting engagement (e.g. by offering support when needed); and (c) nourishing engagement (e.g. celebrating the results) [25]. By undertaking such actions, VT leaders have a greater chance at inciting members' levels of motivation and interest in the project over time [25]. These findings highlight the importance of creating and maintaining a social 'virtual' context [31], which is oftentimes underplayed within the VT environment.

Those at the helm of a VT, and irrespective of leadership style, need to undertake specific actions in order to promote and manage efficacious team working at the different stages of the VT lifecycle. These include creating a social context in the welcoming phase, specifying appropriate use of communication tools in the working phase, and reflecting on experiential learning in the wrapping-up phase. By being culturally conscious and providing tailored feedback, VT leaders can boost their members' sense of pride, motivation and commitment, thus positively impacting their sense of well-being. As it has been suggested,

> Some prefer to be coached and receive positive feedback making them proud of their work (employees in the USA), others prefer frequent

communication and reviews (employees in Spain), want to communicate but not be reviewed (employees in Australia), or supervised but not explicitly be made proud of their work (employees in Japan). [31, p. 231]

10.3 Managing Social Exchanges in VTs

In agile working contexts, new digital technologies emerge constantly, and with them come new team management opportunities and challenges. Social networking sites (SNS) offer the capability to transcend personal and work spheres, and broaden communications from more traditional dyadic exchanges, to multi-person interactions [3]. The above authors make the distinction between enterprise social media used traditionally for work only (e.g. Slack, MS Teams), social media used for personal exchanges only (e.g. Snapchat, dating apps) and other hybrid social media that can be used for work, personal interactions or both (e.g. Twitter and Facebook). SNS, therefore, have the potential to engender new opportunities for VT members, who lack face-to-face (F2F) communication, to access the potentially missing social component of VT teamwork and allow virtual connection to teammates. Enterprise SNS, in particular, influence initial impression formation of VT members who cannot meet F2F in the early stages of the VT lifecycle [9]. This, however, raises questions regarding accuracy of impressions, privacy and boundary management. For example, if VT members are connecting via SNS, does this extend the working day insofar that well-being is negatively impacted? Further, to what extent are teammates happy to share personal information via hybrid media with colleagues, and how appropriate is this?

These issues highlight some of the domains in which future research into VTs should focus. For example, a greater understanding is needed, relating to how ubiquitous connectivity may influence VT members' well-being, especially when work boundaries are transcended via social media and hybrid use of SNS among colleagues. While the issue of ubiquitous connectivity concerns all workers, examining it in the VT context is essential, in order to explore how tools designed to facilitate more social components of work could equally create new problems. The need to examine these issues and other burgeoning trends is outlined now below.

10.4   CURRENT TRENDS AND THREE DIRECTIONS FOR FUTURE VT RESEARCH

As agile working practices continue to gain traction, VTs will continue to be applied and to evolve in the modern work era. Three categories of future research into VTs are therefore highlighted as worth studying, in order to ensure that VTs are optimised as a team structure that can assist workers in working 'well' and with agility. These categories relate to: (a) 'emerging strands': areas that have seen limited attention in the VT literature (creativity, (mis)communication, conflict, boundary-blurring SNS and coordination mechanisms); (b) 'unexplored strands': areas that relate to specific VT characteristics, but have not been explicitly studied (impacts of fluid VT membership, generational impacts); and (c) 'out-of-domain strands': areas that may be popular in other literatures, but have not been studied in the VT context (connectivity, legal context, well-being, work-life boundaries; see [12] for more. While some of these themes, for example those presented in the first category, have been explored to some extent, they feature as fertile areas for future research, often in combination with other topics. For example, conflict (a recognised inhibitor to well-being) could be managed by adopting an adaptation strategy (e.g. interaction avoidance or image-sheltering) [16]. However, further research into conflict in VTs could examine more explicitly the effects of those strategies on well-being or the leader's input in the management of those strategies.

10.5   RECOMMENDATIONS FOR VT LEADERS AND MEMBERS

The study of VTs holds practical significance, and a number of articles have been written for the practitioner community; these are mostly oriented around best practices that could improve leadership [31], virtual teamwork performance [21] communication [13] and trust [24]. These articles urge practitioners to: (a) establish a social context upfront [31] and to stay 'in-sync' with teammates throughout the VT lifecycle [13], as a means for mitigating the negative effects associated with the lack of F2F interaction; (b) use appropriate technologies for different tasks and to embed technology in everyday work [21]; and (c) create a shared identity and common goals that can be used to minimise power imbalances and coercive behaviour [24]. Adding to these principles, in an era of ubiquitous connectivity that may lead to an extension of working hours while working virtually, practitioners should be conscious of their own agency in managing connectivity [18] in a way that helps them to capitalise on the benefits of VTs without leading to violations of their personal work-life boundaries. Chapter 6 further examines the concept of worker agency as a tool for managing new technology in an agile working world.

While the above suggestions are useful, it is important that managers and practitioners identify the characteristics of their own VTs, the challenges associated with them, and the necessary strategies requiring development to help VTs deal with their specific challenges. For example, as discussed above, allowing VTs to be flexible in moving between different members to 'lead' different aspects of the project at different stages in the lifecycle (depending on expertise) can be a useful way of effectively meeting project goals. Allowing members to emerge as leaders based on the goal (rather than on status or formally appointed positions) is likely to lead to more creative and highly performing teams [6]. Additionally, inter-organisational VTs should ensure: (a) that organisational priorities do not take precedent over team priorities; and (b) that terminology and 'language' norms be established for different organisational contexts. Similarly, VT members with limited or no F2F communication could investigate utilising the capabilities of SNS (while establishing acceptable boundary conditions) in order to develop a sustainable social context throughout the VT lifecycle. 'Stronger voices' often seen in physically collocated subgroups [7] may contribute to conflict and negatively influence the well-being of subgroups, or individuals, whose voices cannot be heard. Developing an inclusive and fair VT climate, with similar conditions for all, has been found to reinforce VT members' well-being [1].

10.6   CONCLUSION

The VT literature continues to be a fertile research field. In the past, VTs were seen as boundaryless configurations allowing individuals to work across borders of geography, organisation and time zone. The 'always-on' culture of ubiquitous connectivity introduces a new facet of 'boundarylessness' that sees individuals' work transcend personal and work domains. A multi-disciplinary approach could be useful in tackling some of the issues identified in this chapter, to move the research field forward towards unexplored and out-of-domain strands. To ensure that VT members' well-being is optimised, VT leaders should recognise that there is no one-size-fits-all approach and that leadership style and actions are best aligned to the idiosyncrasies of their teams and projects, bearing in mind that these may need to change as the VT lifecycle evolves. Similarly, VT members could be educated to understand that the flexibility offered by the virtual working environment (e.g. when working from home) should not be experienced at the expense of their well-being or contribute to violation of their own work-life boundaries. An acknowledgement of the need to work in this flexible, ever-evolving and responsive manner epitomises the ethos of agile working.

REFERENCES

1. Adamovic, M. (2018). An employee-focused human resource management perspective for the management of global virtual teams. *The International Journal of Human Resource Management, 29*(14), 2159–2187. https://doi.org/10.1080/09585192.2017.1323227.
2. Angear, S. (2020, March 25). How many people in the UK worked from home prior to Coronavirus outbreak? *Business Leader Magazine.* https://www.businessleader.co.uk/how-many-people-in-the-uk-worked-from-home-prior-to-coronavirus-outbreak/81646/. Accessed 31 March 2020.
3. Archer-Brown, C., Marder, B., Calvard, T., & Kowalski, T. (2018). Hybrid social media: Employees' use of a boundary-spanning technology. *New Technology, Work and Employment, 33*(1), 74–93. https://doi.org/10.1111/ntwe.12103.
4. Bell, B. S., McAlpine, K. L., & Hill, N. S. (2017). Leading from a distance: Advancements in virtual leadership research. In R. N. Landers (Ed.), *The Cambridge handbook of technology and employee behavior.* Cambridge, UK: Cambridge University Press.
5. Chamakiotis, P., Boukis, A., Panteli, N., & Papadopoulos, T. (2020). The role of temporal coordination for the fuzzy front-end of innovation in virtual teams. *International Journal of Information Management, 50,* 182–190. https://doi.org/10.1016/j.ijinfomgt.2019.04.015.
6. Chamakiotis, P., & Panteli, N. (2017). Leading the creative process: The case of virtual product design. *New Technology, Work and Employment, 32*(1), 28–42. https://doi.org/10.1111/ntwe.12081.
7. Chamakiotis, P., Dekoninck, E. A., & Panteli, N. (2013). Factors influencing creativity in virtual design teams: An interplay between technology, teams

and individuals. *Creativity and Innovation Management, 22*(3), 265–279. https://doi.org/10.1111/caim.12039.

8. Chamakiotis, P., & Panteli, N. (2010). E-leadership styles for global virtual teams. In P. Yoong (Ed.), *Leadership in the digital enterprise: Issues and challenges* (pp. 143–161). Hershey, PA, USA: IGI Global. https://doi.org/10.4018/978-1-60566-958-8.ch011.

9. Cummings, J., & Dennis, A. R. (2018). Virtual first impressions matter: The effect of enterprise social networking sites on impression formation in virtual teams. *MIS Quarterly, 42*(3), 697–717. https://doi.org/10.25300/MISQ/2018/13202.

10. Dulebohn, J. H., & Hoch, J. E. (2017). Virtual teams in organizations. *Human Resource Management Review, 27*(4), 569–574. https://doi.org/10.1016/j.hrmr.2016.12.004.

11. Ebrahim, N. A., Ahmed, S., & Taha, Z. (2009). Virtual teams: A literature review. *Australian Journal of Basic and Applied Sciences, 3*(3), 2653–2669. https://doi.org/10.6084/M9.FIGSHARE.103369.

12. Gilson, L. L., Maynard, M. T., Jones Young, N. C., Vartiainen, M., & Hakonen, M. (2015). Virtual teams research: 10 years, 10 themes, and 10 opportunities. *Journal of Management, 41*(5), 1313–1337. https://doi.org/10.1177/0149206314559946.

13. Hill, N. S., & Bartol, K. M. (2018). Five ways to improve communication in virtual teams. *MIT Sloan Management Review, 60*(1), 1–5.

14. Hoegl, M., & Muethel, M. (2016). Enabling shared leadership in virtual project teams: A practitioners' guide. *Project Management Journal, 47*(1), 7–12. https://doi.org/10.1002/pmj.21564.

15. Kolb, D. G. (2008). Exploring the metaphor of connectivity: Attributes, dimensions and duality. *Organization Studies, 29*(1), 127–144. https://doi.org/10.1177/0170840607084574.

16. Lee, J. Y.-H., Panteli, N., Bülow, A. M., & Hsu, C. (2018). Email adaptation for conflict handling: A case study of cross-border inter-organisational partnership in East Asia. *Information Systems Journal, 28*(2), 318–339. https://doi.org/10.1111/isj.12139.

17. Lipnack, J., & Stamps, J. (2000). *Virtual teams: People working across boundaries with technology*. New York: Wiley.

18. MacCormick, J. S., Dery, K., & Kolb, D. G. (2012). Engaged or just connected? Smartphones and employee engagement. *Organizational Dynamics, 41*(3), 194–201. https://doi.org/10.1016/j.orgdyn.2012.03.007.

19. Martins, L. L., Gilson, L. L., & Maynard, M. T. (2004). Virtual teams: What do we know and where do we go from here? *Journal of Management, 30*(6), 805–835. https://doi.org/10.1016/j.jm.2004.05.002.

20. Mazmanian, M., Orlikowski, W. J., & Yates, J. (2013). The autonomy paradox: The implications of mobile email devices for knowledge professionals. *Organization Science, 24*(5), 1337–1357. https://doi.org/10.1287/orsc.1120.0806.
21. Nunamaker, J. F., Jr., Reinig, B. A., & Briggs, R. O. (2009). Principles for effective virtual teamwork. *Communications of the ACM, 52*(4), 113–117. https://doi.org/10.1145/1498765.1498797.
22. Ocker, R. J. (2005). Influences on creativity in asynchronous virtual teams: A qualitative analysis of experimental teams. *IEEE Transactions on Professional Communication, 48*(1), 22–39. https://doi.org/10.1109/TPC.2004.843294.
23. Panteli, N., & Davison, R. M. (2005). The role of subgroups in the communication patterns of global virtual teams. *IEEE Transactions on Professional Communication, 48*(2), 191–200. https://doi.org/10.1109/TPC.2005.849651.
24. Panteli, N., & Tucker, R. (2009). Power and trust in global virtual teams. *Communications of the ACM, 52*(12), 113–115. https://doi.org/10.1145/1610252.1610282.
25. Panteli, N., Yalabik, Z. Y., & Rapti, A. (2019). Fostering work engagement in geographically-dispersed and asynchronous virtual teams. *Information Technology & People, 32*(1), 2–17. https://doi.org/10.1108/ITP-04-2017-0133.
26. Schmidt, K., & Bannon, L. (1992). Taking CSCW seriously: Supporting articulation work. *Computer Supported Cooperative Work (CSCW), 1*(1–2), 7–40. https://doi.org/10.1007/978-1-84800-068-1_3.
27. Taras, V., Baack, D., Caprar, D., Dow, D., Froese, F., Jimenez, A., et al. (2019). Diverse effects of diversity: Disaggregating effects of diversity in global virtual teams. *Journal of International Management, 25*(4), 100689. https://doi.org/10.1016/j.intman.2019.100689.
28. Walther, J. B. (1996). Computer-mediated communication: Impersonal, interpersonal, and hyperpersonal interaction. *Communication Research, 23*(1), 3–43. https://doi.org/10.1177/009365096023001001.
29. Watson-Manheim, M. B., Chudoba, K. M., & Crowston, K. (2002). Discontinuities and continuities: A new way to understand virtual work. *Information Technology & People, 15*(3), 191–209. https://doi.org/10.1108/09593840210444746.
30. Yeow, J. (2014). Boundary management in an ICT-enabled project-based organising context. *New Technology, Work and Employment, 29*(3), 237–252. https://doi.org/10.1111/ntwe.12036.
31. Zander, L., Zettinig, P., & Mäkelä, K. (2013). Leading global virtual teams to success. *Organizational Dynamics, 42*(3), 228–237. https://doi.org/10.1016/j.orgdyn.2013.06.008.

CHAPTER 11

Leading and Managing the Occupational Well-Being and Health of Distributed Workers

Rachel Nayani

Abstract In an agile working world, an increasing number of workers spend some of their work time away from a main office or location (i.e. distributed workers). Leading the well-being and health of these workers can be challenging, due to less opportunity for face-to-face contact and potential issues of access to health and well-being-related resources. This chapter reports on a study that identifies leadership frameworks relevant to the distributed work context, as well as management resources which, when utilised, can enhance worker well-being outcomes. Findings have informed the production of practical guidance for line managers and occupational health and well-being practitioners (i.e. professionals tasked with organisational responsibility for worker health and well-being), to use to improve outcomes for distributed workers.

Keywords Distributed workers · Well-being · Leadership · Management

R. Nayani (✉)
University of East Anglia, Norwich, UK
e-mail: r.nayani@uea.ac.uk

C. Grant and E. Russell (eds.), *Agile Working and Well-Being in the Digital Age*, https://doi.org/10.1007/978-3-030-60283-3_11

11.1   INTRODUCTION

In this chapter, we explore the challenges for facilitating (and moni-toring) the well-being of workers who are out of sight of their manager for some of their work time (i.e. distributed workers). A distributed worker is a particular 'type' of agile worker in that they can be defined as not working from traditional office-based locations, instead spending at least part of their time working outdoors, at the premises of other organisations or from home. As distributed workers are dispersed, they rely on communications technologies and line managers to guide them in meeting their work and organisational goals. The extent to which a distributed worker follows agile work practices (such as embracing digital technology) varies according to occupation and infrastructure. Yet, even in traditionally so-called blue-collar work, distributed workers are required to digitally 'connect' at least some of the time. In this chapter, optimising the well-being of distributed workers is considered, by focusing on (i) the leadership provided by their managers, (ii) the support/practices/guidance that organisations can put in place, and (iii) actions that can be taken by workers themselves. Recommendations are provided for managers, practitioners, researchers and workers, to help manage and promote the occupational health and well-being of distributed workers.

11.1.1   Relevance of This Topic to the Phenomenon of Agile Working

When employees work away from their main location for certain periods, they are referred to as 'distributed workers' [5]. Distributed workers are found in a wide range of non-office-based occupations (e.g. construc-tion, utilities and emergency services). However, as organisations seek the benefits of spatial and temporal flexibility associated with agile work, there is also a trend towards multi-locational working in non-traditional distributed working roles (i.e. office-based occupations); indeed, the glob-ally distributed workforce is around 40% of the total workforce as of 2020 [23].

Although distributed working enables flexibility, a lack of physical and temporal proximity between workers and managers poses several chal-lenges for organisations in ensuring the well-being of these workers. Firstly, there is less opportunity for face-to-face interaction to identify well-being-related issues, observe employees, provide timely feedback and advice or facilitate leadership role-modelling around self-management of well-being [5]. Secondly, distributed workers have fewer opportunities to informally exchange of well-being-related information (i.e. with work colleagues), infrequent access to organisational information, and may be unable to access and communicate with organisational decision-makers when advice and support is needed [5]. Thirdly, distributed working provides less access to structures that promote health and well-being [5]. Finally, many distributed work settings, such as those in health, community and social care, present psychological hazards and risks [4] that may in turn generate adverse well-being.

In the light of these challenges, it is becoming increasingly important to understand what factors influence good well-being and health outcomes, as distributed workers seek to achieve organisational goals. Two such factors are (i) the leadership styles adopted by those responsible for workers, and (ii) the practices, procedures and systems used by managers to facilitate worker well-being, health and safety [15]. Yet, although leadership and management are equally important influences on good well-being, health and safety outcomes [20], in the past, research has tended to focus only on specific leadership frameworks, on narrow and distinct aspects of management, such as regulatory compliance [20] or managerial empathy [22], or on employees in fixed locations.

Leadership is generally viewed as a relationship between a leader and follower, comprising behaviours that are directed at facilitating and influencing desired outcomes, including good well-being [25]. Leaders are a potentially powerful influence in modelling positive behaviours, rewarding and encouraging desirable behaviours and activities, and making decisions that enhance workers' experiences and/or minimise stressors [11]. Several general leadership frameworks are associated with positive worker outcomes. Transformational leadership [2] is arguably the most dominant framework, in which leaders inspire workers to higher levels of motivation and performance by setting a compelling vision, serving as a role model, offering challenge and demonstrating genuine concern for individuals. Whereas transformational leadership seeks to inspire followers, the transactional leadership [1] framework focuses on the exchange of tangible rewards for the productive work and loyalty of workers. The relationship between leaders and subordinates itself is the focus of the leader-member exchange (LMX) framework [9], which posits that leaders tailor their approach to the worker and the worker context. Traditional leadership frameworks (such as those outlined above) have been developed by applying the assumption of face-to face interaction, potentially rendering these less useful in ensuring the well-being and health of distributed workers. Furthermore, in practice, pluralist approaches to leadership (i.e. combinations of styles) may be more suited to the range of leadership activities undertaken to manage agile working, rendering single leadership framework(s) potentially redundant [20]. Similarly, although management systems, procedures and practices are an important influence upon the worker experience, research has been fragmented and lacks a coherent heuristic framework to aid our understanding of the role of management on worker well-being.

Therefore, specific attention is required as to when, whether and how existing leadership styles, combinations of styles and/or management approaches are suited to the distributed work context. This is especially important to consider from a health and well-being perspective as distributed working encompasses a number of risks that may not beset non-distributed workers. For example, distributed workers are more susceptible to (i) feelings of social isolation, (ii) physical risks arising from unpredictable or dangerous work contexts, and (iii) risks associated with location-switching. In the following sections, the health and well-being-oriented findings of a study commissioned by the Institution of Occupational Safety and Health (IOSH), and undertaken by the author and colleagues, are reported on.

11.2   RELEVANT LITERATURE
AND THEORETICAL FRAMEWORKS

11.2.1   Leadership Frameworks Relevant to the Distributed Working Context

A review of the literature, pertinent to well-being and health-related leadership for distributed workers [16], found that existing research was limited and there were no leadership frameworks developed specifically for the distributed work context. However, research has identified three existing leadership frameworks that may be applicable to the distributed work context. These are outlined now below.

Focusing on the interactional exchanges between manager and workers as encapsulated by the LMX framework [7], the authors found that positive relationships between manager and worker were associated with positive outcomes such as job satisfaction and safety-oriented behaviours.

Other research [16] found that 'considerate' leadership facilitated a greater involvement of distributed workers in the workplace and higher levels of satisfaction with their supervisors. Considerate leadership is a specific leadership style, which aligns to the individualised consideration dimension of transformational leadership, whereby the leader focuses on relational elements such as generating trust and respect. Finally, the quality of the leader-follower relationship, in particular relating to trust and personal recognition, was related to worker motivation, safety behaviours and positive well-being, when examined through the lens of the transformational leadership framework [2, 24]. Each of these frameworks is significant for effectively leading distributed workers because the social/relational nature of the leader-follower relationship is foregrounded. The frameworks emphasise how the leader prioritises concern for their worker, in relation to their health and well-being. These are key features, often overlooked in distributed work, because of the remote and often less visible proximity of the worker, to their leader.

11.2.2   *Management Resources Relevant to the Distributed Working Context*

Management comprises facilitating means [15], such as systems, practices and procedures, to oversee worker activity. A useful heuristic for understanding how organisations enable individual outcomes (i.e. well-being) is through the notion of 'resources' [10]. A review of the literature [17] identified two main types of resources applicable to the distributed work context: structural resources and manager deployment resources. Each will be outlined now below.

Structural resources refer to tangible assets (or means), such as technologies that enable connectivity between distributed workers and their organisation. Examples include technology-enabled communications with managers or colleagues (e.g. via email, messaging or video call) and technology-enabled information such procedures, policies and training materials via the organisation intranet. Due to their spatial and temporal distance, distributed workers are more reliant on structural resources compared with office or single-location workers. Structural resources play an important role by providing distributed workers with (i) important information such as promoting good well-being and health-related behaviours, and (ii) communications, that provide managerial advice and role clarity [17]. Yet, while playing an important facilitating role, the application of structural resources by workers and their managers is more important than frequency of use [16, 19]. Lack of clarity over roles and desired behaviours is a source of stress for distributed workers [17], whereas positive worker outcomes, such as job satisfaction, arise when managers communicate motivating language and provide clear instructions [13]. Even when organisational well-being-related information or technology-enabled communications are available, managers either lack the knowledge of how to utilise this or do not utilise this [12].

Further, manager deployment of resources (the way in which the line manager is deployed or put to action as a manager) is applicable to the distributed work context in two ways. Firstly, positive worker outcomes, such as job satisfaction, are found when the line manager has an understanding of the nature of distributed work, such as if the manager is also a distributed worker [6]. Conversely, a lack of understanding by the line manager is associated with adverse well-being, such as conflicting and unrealistic expectations and increased workload [14]. Secondly, line manager support and encouragement reduces adverse outcomes for workers undergoing demanding work, while conversely, a lack of support is associated with adverse well-being and health outcomes [3]. Notably, the literature review also found that, despite often holding pivotal organisational roles, very little attention has been paid to the role of occupational health and well-being practitioners (i.e. people tasked by organisations to support well-being) in developing procedures, policies and initiatives, as well as advising organisational decision-makers [17]. Thus, more is needed to understand how managers' deployment of resources may operate in practice, and whether different professionals can contribute differently to worker well-being, depending on their respective roles.

In summary, from past literature, in ensuring good well-being and health of distributed workers, existing leadership styles may be applicable. However, management resources, such as the availability and use of technology-enabled communications (structural resources), as well as managerial understanding of distributed work and support provided to workers, come into play. The limited research into leadership and management approaches for distributed worker well-being highlighted by the literature review has prompted an empirical study, which is described in the following sections.

11.3   Examining Well-Being and Health-Related Leadership and Management of Distributed Workers: An Empirical Study

Given the lack of research attention given to leadership frameworks specific to the distributed work context, and the need for a coherent integration of management, a mixed method study with two phases was undertaken [18]. The study examined leadership behaviours and management resources applicable in the distributed work context. In phase one, interviews with eleven experts and 41 occupational safety and health (OSH) practitioners from 19 organisations explored the important leadership behaviours and management resources for the distributed work context. Content analysis and mapping techniques identified pertinent leadership behaviours from existing frameworks, along with enablers and challenges of good health and well-being for the distributed work context. Data informed the survey design for phase two [18].

Analysis of phase one interview data revealed the leadership behaviours that enable worker well-being and health could be mapped to the transformational leadership framework [2], the transactional leadership framework (via contingent reward behaviours: [21]) and the LMX framework (via the trust element: [8]). For example, the following interview extract illustrates the role-modelling aspect of transformational leadership: *'you have got to be seen to practice what you preach... so it's making sure that my team, managers, supervisors lead by example'* (OSH practitioner, Utilities Sector). Similarly, the following extract exemplifies an emphasis on interpersonal relationships as encapsulated the LMX framework: *'That is one of the issues with all distributed workers, that interconnection on a personal level with a supervisor or manager who knows you and who actually maybe has some personal connection with you'* (OSH practitioner, Transport Sector [18]).

Behaviours could also be linked to a scale of health-specific leadership [9], specifically the line manager coaching workers in how to manage their health and conveying the importance the organisation places upon worker health.

Analysis of interview data highlighted structural resources as important enablers for distributed workers' well-being and health, but only in tandem with good leadership. Resources that enabled good well-being comprised: information communications technology, access to information about healthy working, training and promotion of well-being and health policies, as well as supporting procedures and monitoring processes. Resources that presented the greatest challenges included access to support, advice and the line manager, especially when workers worked away from a main location for long periods of time, or moved between physical locations (i.e. switched between modes of distributed working).

The phase two survey was conducted to build upon the findings of the interview study. The aim of the survey was to assess leadership behaviours identified as important in the interview study and identify the role of management resources in ensuring the health and well-being of distributed workers. A multi-level survey was administered to 822 distributed workers, 112 line managers and 40 OSH practitioners, across nineteen organisations, predominantly working in higher risk environments [18]. The survey involved distributed workers rating their line manager's leadership behaviours, their own well-being and health outcomes, and how they personally utilised enabling management resources (as per the findings from phase one). Line managers reported on their own well-being and their use of management resources. The survey also probed the leadership that the organisational OSH practitioner provided to line managers, in order to explore whether leadership was role-modelled; both line manager and OSH practitioner reported on the OSH practitioner's leadership behaviours.

Findings from the survey were twofold revealing the role of the line manager but also that of the organisation.

11.3.1   The Role of the Line Manager: Leadership Frameworks Applicable to the Distributed Work Context

Analysis revealed that the existing leadership frameworks identified in the interview study are applicable to the distributed work context and linked to increased worker health and well-being. The leadership styles are specifically those encapsulated by: transformational leadership, the contingent reward element of transactional leadership; the trust element of LMX; and adapted health-specific leadership. The trust element of LMX in particular was linked to health outcomes in all cases, whereas health-related leadership had stronger associations with outcomes of integration, knowledge exchange and technology-mediated communications. The strongest relationships between line managers' leadership behaviours and worker outcomes were found to relate to transformational leadership and LMX [18]. Therefore, in ensuring well-being and health outcomes for distributed workers, findings suggest that there is utility in line managers adopting an integrated approach that takes on board elements from these leadership styles.

Furthermore, findings revealed a lack of association between outcomes and leadership at the group level, whereas significant outcomes across a range of well-being and health indicators were detected at the individual level of analysis. This suggests that effects of leadership on worker well-being and health outcomes occur through personal experiences between the distributed worker and their line manager, rather than through experiences common to group members, thereby highlighting the importance of individualised and quality relations between manager and worker. Hence, findings suggest that the need for good interpersonal relations (i.e. mutual trust) and clear expectations are heightened when workers work autonomously and remotely from their manager.

11.3.2   The Role of Organisational Well-Being and Health-Oriented Practitioners

According to the survey results, line managers did not role model the leadership behaviours of their OSH practitioner [18]. Therefore, the study found no evidence for a cascade of leadership role modelling from OSH practitioner, to manager to worker. Rather, unlike the line manager, who exercises influence through a dyadic relationship with their workers, the study found that OSH practitioners exercised their influence at the group level, for example, by providing information at group meetings, via information communications technology and through activities that are related to the promotion of well-being and health. Thus, OSH practitioners have an instrumental role to play in providing well-being-related information to support a remote and/or autonomous workforce.

11.3.3   Utilisation of Management Resources

The phase two survey analysis explored the extent to which enabling resources such as training, information and communications were associated with the leadership of line managers. Findings are that utilisation of resources was associated with better manager-worker relationships, which enhanced worker outcomes. For example, line managers reporting appropriate health and well-being-related training and engaging in health-specific leadership behaviours had better relationships with their distributed workers [18]. Conversely, line managers holding fewer health and well-being-related meetings and less monitoring of workers' well-being and safety had poorer relationships with their workers. Therefore, the line manager's utilisation of resources is an important facet of distributed worker well-being and health. These findings suggest that in agile work, enabling resources are of particular importance in supporting worker well-being to compensate for the lack the immediacy of information and communications when compared to an organisational setting. Furthermore, line managers who do not fully engage in, for example, monitoring worker well-being and forging good relationships may inhibit worker well-being. Therefore, the way the line manager is deployed in their role should be considered part of the resources landscape.

Overall, findings suggest that the line manager and OSH practitioner play important complementary roles in facilitating the well-being and health of distributed workers. The line manager does so through dyadic leadership behaviours with their workers, and the use of enabling management resources. Meanwhile, the OSH practitioner plays a role in generating resources, raising awareness and encouraging worker and manager participation in organisational well-being and health-related activities. However, more needs to be done for line managers to apply the appropriate leadership behaviours and to implement the enabling resources (e.g. via training and awareness building).

11.4   PRACTICAL IMPLICATIONS

Following this research [18], the authors converted the findings into a practice-oriented toolkit, suitable for organisations, OSH practitioners and line managers. The toolkit centred on a leadership behavioural framework for managers of distributed workers, and a self-reflection framework for health and well-being-oriented practitioners.

The line manager behavioural framework encompassed the relevant leadership behaviours and comprised self- and other-ratings through which line managers assessed their leadership behaviours and identified opportunities for personal development, such as training in relevant types of leadership. As the research found that the OSH practitioner's influence lay in providing, for example, information and guidance, and playing a facilitating role in supporting line managers, the practitioner self-assessment framework set out the key skills underpinning these activities. These skills were identified as: getting the message across, listening to and understanding distributed workers and their role; empowering and collaborating; and cascading knowledge and support to workers, via managers [18]. Both frameworks provide practical guiding principles and self-assessment for those responsible for distributed worker well-being and health.

11.5   Limitations in the Field and Implications for Future Research

Although distributed working encompasses a wide range of occupations, there are common characteristics that generate challenges for organisations. The studies of [17, 18] highlight the merits of taking a broad approach, by examining a range of leadership styles, and management resources to facilitate worker well-being and health. This approach differs from prior research that has examined single occupations or a narrow range of leadership or management influences.

Furthermore, the study highlighted the complementary but distinct roles of the line manager and OSH practitioner in ensuring good worker outcomes. There is a lack of research into the role of the OSH practitioner in ensuring good worker outcomes, suggesting an area for future research. Additionally, the study did not find that line managers modelled leadership behaviours of their OSH practitioner [18]; it may be that line managers take their role-modelling cues from their own line manager instead. Given the importance of enacting such behaviours, future research could examine why line managers may not role-model practitioner leadership behaviours.

11.6   Key Learning and Recommendations

The research of [18] has focused attention on the key individuals responsible for ensuring good outcomes for distributed workers, by highlighting the important behaviours and the management resources that may be utilised. The study had a strong practical focus, in generating a toolkit to help organisational decision-makers improve their approaches to distributed worker health and well-being. Furthermore, the research shows that, despite encompassing a wide range of occupations, there are sufficiently common characteristics of distributed working to merit multi-sector research of concepts that are applicable to all work contexts, such as leadership and management.

11.7   CONCLUSION

In this chapter, the challenges of attending to the well-being and health needs of distributed workers were outlined. The extent to which distributed workers follow agile work practices varies (i.e. so-called blue-collar workers may be less likely to undertake agile working). Distributed work is characterised by spatial and/or temporal distance between workers and managers; the research outlined above has direct implications for agile working contexts, specifically relating to how leaders and line managers can enable resources to support the well-being of workers who are out of sight. Furthermore, the role of OSH practitioners was identified as pivotal in supporting line managers, for example, by generating and promoting well-being-relevant information, facilitating training and establishing procedures.

REFERENCES

1. Bass, B. M. (1985). *Leadership and performance beyond expectations*. New York: Free Press.
2. Bass, B. M., & Riggio, R. E. (2006). *Transformational leadership*. Mahwah, NJ: Lawrence Erlbaum Associates Publishers.
3. Chen, W. Q., Wong, T. W., & Yu, I. T. (2008). Association of occupational stress and social support with health-related behaviors among Chinese offshore oil workers. *Journal of Occupational Health, 50*(3), 262–269. https://doi.org/10.1539/joh.l7149.
4. Danna, K., & Griffin, R. (1999). Health and well-being in the workplace: A review and synthesis of the literature. *Journal of Management, 25*(3), 357–384. https://doi.org/10.1177/014920639902500305.
5. Dix, A. J., & Beale, R. (1996). Information requirements of distributed workers. In A. J. Dix & R. Beale (Eds.), *Remote cooperation: CSCW issues for mobile and teleworkers* (pp. 113–143). New York: Springer. https://doi.org/10.1007/978-1-4471-1496-3_10.
6. Golden, T. D., & Fromen, A. (2011). Does it matter where your manager works? Comparing managerial work mode (traditional, telework, virtual) across subordinate work experiences and outcomes. *Human Relations, 64*(11), 1451–1475. https://doi.org/10.1177/0018726711418387.

7. Golden, T. D., & Veiga, J. F. (2008). The impact of superior–subordinate relationships on the commitment, job satisfaction, and performance of virtual workers. *The Leadership Quarterly, 19*(1), 77–88. https://doi.org/10.1016/j.leaqua.2007.12.009.

8. Graen, G. B., & Uhl-Bien, M. (1995). Relationship-based approach to leadership: Development of leader-member exchange (LMX) theory of leadership over 25 years: Applying a multi-level multi-domain perspective. *The Leadership Quarterly, 6*(2), 219–247. https://doi.org/10.1016/1048-984 3(95)90036-5.

9. Gurt, J., Schwennen, C., & Elke, G. (2011). Health-specific leadership: Is there an association between leader consideration for the health of employees and their strain and well-being? *Work & Stress, 25*(2), 108–127. https://doi.org/10.1080/02678373.2011.595947.

10. Hobfoll, S. E. (1989). Conservation of resources: A new attempt at conceptualizing stress. *American Psychologist, 44*(3), 513–524. https://doi.org/10.1037/0003-066X.44.3.513.

11. Kelloway, E. K., & Barling, J. (2010). Leadership development as an intervention in occupational health psychology. *Work & Stress, 24*(3), 260–279. https://doi.org/10.1080/02678373.2010.518441.

12. Konradt, U., Schmook, R., Wilm, A., & Hertel, G. (2000). Health circles for teleworkers: Selective results on stress, strain and coping styles. *Health Education Research, 15*(3), 327–338. https://doi.org/10.1093/her/15.3.327.

13. Madlock, P. E. (2013). The influence of motivational language in the technologically mediated realm of telecommuters. *Human Resource Management Journal, 23*(2), 196–210. https://doi.org/10.1111/j.1748-8583.2012.001 91.x.

14. Mihhailova, G., Õun, K., & Türk, K. (2011). Virtual work usage and challenges in different service sector branches. *Baltic Journal of Management, 6*(3), 342–356. https://doi.org/10.1108/17465261111167984.

15. Mintzberg, H. (2004). *Managers, not MBAs: A hard look at the soft practice of managing and management development*. San Francisco: Berrett-Koehler Publishers.

16. Mulki, J. P., & Jaramillo, F. (2011). Workplace isolation: Salespeople and supervisors in USA. *The International Journal of Human Resource Management, 22*(4), 902–923. https://doi.org/10.1080/09585192.2011.555133.

17. Nayani, R. J., Nielsen, K., Daniels, K., Donaldson-Feilder, E. J., & Lewis, R. C. (2018). Out of sight and out of mind? A literature review of occupational safety and health leadership and management of distributed workers. *Work & Stress, 32*(2), 124–146. https://doi.org/10.1080/02678373.2017.139 0797.

18. Nielsen, K., Daniels, K., Nayani, R., Donaldson-Feilder, E., & Lewis, R. (2017). *Out of sight, out of mind? Research into the occupational safety and health of distributed workers.* IOSH. https://iosh.com/outofsight. Accessed 10 August 2020.
19. Nurmi, N. (2011). Coping with coping strategies: How distributed teams and their members deal with the stress of distance, time zones and culture. *Stress and Health, 27*(2), 123–143. https://doi.org/10.1002/smi.1327.
20. Pilbeam, C., Doherty, N., Davidson, R., & Denyer, D. (2016). Safety leadership practices for organizational safety compliance: Developing a research agenda from a review of the literature. *Safety Science, 86,* 110–121. https://doi.org/10.1016/j.ssci.2016.02.015.
21. Podsakoff, P. M., MacKenzie, S. B., Moorman, R. H., & Fetter, R. (1990). Transformational leader behaviors and their effects on followers' trust in leader, satisfaction, and organizational citizenship behaviors. *The Leadership Quarterly, 1*(2), 107–142. https://doi.org/10.1016/1048-9843(90)90009-7.
22. Scott, B. A., Colquitt, J. A., Paddock, E. L., & Judge, T. A. (2010). A daily investigation of the role of manager empathy on employee well-being. *Organizational Behavior and Human Decision Processes, 113*(2), 127–140. https://doi.org/10.1016/j.obhdp.2010.08.001.
23. Strategy Analytics. (2015). *Global mobile workforce forecast, 2015–2020.* https://www.strategyanalytics.com/access-services/enterprise/mobile-workforce/market-data/report-detail/global-mobile-workforce-forecast-2015-2020. Accessed 10 August 2020.
24. Whitford, T., & Moss, S. A. (2009). Transformational leadership in distributed work groups: The moderating role of follower regulatory focus and goal orientation. *Communication Research, 36*(6), 810–837. https://doi.org/10.1177/0093650209346800.
25. Yukl, G., Gordon, A., & Taber, T. (2002). A hierarchical taxonomy of leadership behavior: Integrating a half century of behavior research. *Journal of Leadership & Organizational Studies, 9*(1), 15–32. https://doi.org/10.1177/107179190200900102.

CHAPTER 12

The Case of Co-working Spaces for Fulfilling Agile Working and Worker Needs

Alessandra Mossa

Abstract In an era dominated by information and communication technologies, that have made work ubiquitous and potentially boundaryless, the rise of *co-working spaces* has constituted a counterintuitive example of a revised interest in the role of space and co-location for achieving working identity, a sense of belonging, collaboration and innovation. This rise is also part of a general shift towards a more meaningful and agile idea of work. The rationale behind the rise and success of co-working spaces may emblematically infer that physical co-presence and co-location still matter, despite being made potentially redundant by digital technologies. This chapter will assess the pros and cons of co-working practices and aims to identify what elements could benefit both individuals and organizations in future agile working.

Keywords COVID-19 · Homeworking · Co-working ·
Future of the office · Co-location · Work-life boundaries

A. Mossa (✉)
University of Sussex, Brighton, UK
e-mail: A.Mossa@sussex.ac.uk

12.1   Introduction

In the twenty-first century, the ongoing scaling back of welfare states, accompanied by the widespread encouragement of more "entrepreneurial" and private responses to public needs, has contributed to a gradual atomization of work. This has thrown independent workers and small start-ups into a state of permanent precariousness, at both the lower and higher ends of the income scale [30, 35, 41]. In this context, informal and precarious working practices, such as sharing office facilities on a temporal basis or using "third places" like coffee shops and libraries as a workplace [28], have not only been pitched as inevitable to survival, but have been celebrated as the bottom-up response to both the increasing unaffordability of office space and the feeling of alienation that homeworking can imply [22].

The rise of co-working has represented a particular territorial expression of the digital economy and a re-territorialisation of the digital nomad/agile worker who, through this flexible working arrangement, has found a way to defeat isolation and an eroded working identity [9, 12]. Co-working practices suggest that the need for co-presence and face-to-face interaction is resistant to the geographical dispersion enabled by information and communication technologies [24]. Co-working today exists across a wide spectrum of price levels and represents one of the spatial and social infrastructures of the new economy. It is representative of a behavioural and socio-economic shift that emphasises accessibility over ownership, flexibility and mobility over stability [22]. However, it is also presented as a conscious rationalisation of some of the pathologies of economic crises, identifying precarity and lack of permanent office space as conscious lifestyle choices [39]; de facto contributing to make new working arrangements permanently precarious [23, 36, 41].

Against the backdrop of this burgeoning trend towards co-working, in 2020 the COVID-19 pandemic forced people to stay at home and made remote working a reality for the majority of knowledge workers around the world. As central business districts in cities laid empty and more people began working from their kitchen tables, a great deal of speculation about the end of the traditional office began to dominate the public discourse [4]. In conjunction with this, the co-working sector began to experience obvious financial difficulties, as demand for shared office space was halted. Yet, despite its extremely fragile business model (mainly based on short-term leases), in post-pandemic time, co-working seems to offer the degree of flexibility that many organisations and individuals will be looking to access in the future [10]. This is especially likely if the demise of the 'traditional office' continues to gain traction, with commuter-weary, precarious and entrepreneurial workers, along with post-COVID homeworking zealots, all looking for opportunities to work both remotely and communally—potentially in more local settings.

Through this chapter, the implications of organising agile working via co-working spaces for both organisations and independent workers will be explored. In particular, the focus will be on how co-working spaces impact physical and spatial work-life boundaries, and satisfy human needs for work identification, creativity, collaboration and a sense of belonging.

12.2   Home-Office or Office-Home?

As a result of the worldwide lockdown in 2020, the biggest *working-from-home* experiment unexpectedly took place. Suddenly, the implications of homeworking, envisioned in the telecommuting literature since the 1970s [25], became the norm for the majority of knowledge workers and employers, even across sectors that were reluctant—or inadequately equipped—to adopt telework (e.g. public sector, education, etc.) [29]. During the 'experiment', both the potential and limitations of a fully remote working society were realised [26]. Because lockdown meant that other family/friends were also working from home, the pros and cons of co-living and co-working practices were directly experienced for the first time for many people. The boundaries between work and free time, family and work responsibilities, household duties and leisure, private and public sphere were eroded and condensed within the single physical space of the home (see also Chapter 3). Homes were revealed to be unfit for purpose, especially in dense urban settings, when that purpose was reconfigured as needing to provide a suitable space to both work and live [15, 40]. Contextually, virtual platforms replaced face-to-face meetings and allowed working collaboration without any spatio-temporal constraints (wi-fi or 4G permitting), bringing work into the home in a way never before experienced on such a scale [27]. Early reports suggested that this work-home 'revolution' resulted in no loss in worker productivity and efficiency and accompanied a generalised sense of satisfaction from workers [11]. This gave rise to the question as to whether—post-pandemic—agile working could become the new preference, and the new norm, for the majority of knowledge workers. Yet remote working is neither new nor a 'fad'. Pre-pandemic, as a result of rapid technological innovation, work had moved beyond the traditional spatial and temporal boundaries of the office, increasingly contributing to changes in the nature of office space and work style [28, 42]. Advances in information communication technology (ICT) and the consequent rise of more dispersed and remote working practices have given rise to always more flexible and hybrid working arrangements [13, 16, 31].

The increase tendency for an integration of work and leisure and the blurred work/non-work boundaries that post-industrial work incentivises find in co-working one of its spatial manifestations. The global pandemic, all of a sudden, brought our work in our home. The success of co-working, by bringing our homes into the workplace, constitutes the attempt of the market of satisfying the "compulsion of proximity" [24] manifested by remote workers [37].

12.3   Co-working Movement

The first informal and locally based co-working practices can be traced back to the 1990s, when derelict warehouses and redundant flats in cities like London were informally repurposed as ateliers/workspace by creative professionals keen to share costs and basic facilities (e.g. kitchen, printer, tables, wi-fi, etc.). The first wave of co-working arrangements was locally based, small in scale and mainly driven by issues of economic sustainability; it implied a genuine, often pre-existing, collaboration and attracted professions for which collaboration was traditionally achieved through co-presence (e.g. film-making, architecture, design, fashion, etc.) [20].

Starting from the mid-2000s, a gradual corporatisation and commodification of this arrangement has seen co-working providers like Wework expanding worldwide to become an appealing (and expensive) working option for the so-called creative classes. The creative classes are made up of freelancers and start-ups whom Richard Florida considers to be the main and controversial economic drivers of post-industrial cities [8]. These creative classes are an educated, flexible and highly technological workforce who share economic interests and lifestyles and who, thanks to the proliferation of this new urban practice, have gained both visibility and a sense of belonging [37].

The second wave of co-working combined extreme flexibility, in terms of space (hot-desking, multifunctional spaces, hybrid uses) and tenancy, with a strong community vibe. From monthly rented hot-desks to annual leases for private offices, together with a series of working and recreational facilities (conferences rooms, concierges, ping pong tables, open bars, etc.) and the organisation of professional as well as social events, characterise second wave co-working. This offers the physical and digital infrastructure where people with common interests meet and work and leisure activities overlap [9, 22]. These types of spatial arrangements are representative of a "neo-corporate" [10] strategy to use the concept of community, flexibility and happiness as managerial and marketing devices, where spatial arrangements become instrumental in the embodiment of a collective sense of identity that young professionals are looking for [2, 32, 33]. In contrast to the employer that reshapes its workplace according to its employees' needs and taste (e.g., Google, Facebook, etc.), companies like Wework have turned a hybrid workspace and a particular idea of work into a commodity. By providing a hybrid and vibrant working arrangement that mutually encompasses working from home, café and traditional office cultures, Wework has updated the aesthetic of the office and created a counterculture working environment that especially appeals to the boundaryless millennial [12, 34]. Related to this, big corporations, in order to attract and retain young talent, have started to rent this kind of office space for their staff [6].

Neo-corporate co-working targets a particular personality type that is willing to socialise and gives economic value to social relations, seen nowadays as work-related leisure [1, 38]. The workspace appears to have become a 'stage' for such personalities, on which perpetual networking is performed and where everyone is constantly on-script, by being involved in a continuous emotional, performative and aesthetic labour that people hardly recognise as work [5, 43]. The risk is then turning a workplace into the set of an artificially manufactured representation of communal and 'playful' work that is supposedly creating the spatial and social conditions for nurturing innovation and collaboration [3]. In reality, such space is arguably functioning as a mere mechanism for real-estate PR. Co-working providers label their users as 'members', rather than 'tenants'. Yet, in the *neo-corporate* wave of co-working, these members are mostly paying subjects of a prefabricated, romanticised and often exclusive idea of community, where the concept of creativity and collaboration is often a fallacy, rarely tailored to fit personal or professional differences [17, 37].

12.4   Bringing Some Boundaries Back

A wide range of literature has already problematised the blurring of lines between work and free time, the public and the private sphere, and the subsequent risks of reduced work-life balance and well-being. However, little has been said on the role that spatial arrangements play in either accelerating or containing this encroachment [2, 7]. Homeworking can undermine the balance between work and life via the fragmentation of time and tasks that excessive overlapping of activities exacerbates. Having a separate workplace helps: (i) tackle family conflicts, (ii) create a routine, (iii) clarify working identity and (iv) enable a clear transition between work and home time/private and working space. Yet, this is not enough [31]. The relationship between work and leisure time cannot be delineated by the mere separation of workplace alone. Workspaces like Wework, where there is the incentive to find pleasure in work, further blend the distinction between what one perceives as a paid, or payable, activity and what instead is a voluntary one, with obvious implications of self-exploitation [14, 18, 21]. On the other hand, bringing work into the home space (even when spatial arrangements are distinguished) can sully both the work and home-life experience. Further, the opportunities for networking, collaboration, socialisation and mutual learning in the home space are impoverished (even with the advent of virtual video-based meeting sites).

Post-COVID enthusiasm for remote working should not underestimate the offloading of costs onto individuals that going fully agile may generate (e.g. work-from-home IT infrastructure, finding private extra space, virtual miscommunication issues, isolation, lack of visibility, etc.) [35]. Weighted against these costs is the need to value the role of co-presence in creating a sense of belonging, work identity, creativity and collaboration; even though these features may have been manipulated and commodified by neo-corporate co-working. Co-location and co-presence are not inherently sufficient in fostering working collaboration, identity and creativity [19, 37] beyond the will and ethos of users and providers. Within the same job, there are some tasks that are better accomplished alone that demand privacy/no distractions and other tasks that, by benefitting from co-presence and interaction, are best achieved in open spaces [19]. Researchers now face the challenge of recognising and monitoring both individual and organisational differences in the costs and benefits afforded by co-working, homeworking and traditional office working.

This knowledge is needed to inform guidelines (design, behaviours, workers' rights, etc.) regarding the socio-economic, spatial and technological restructuring needed to organise work in the post-pandemic era.

Hybrid remote working arrangements, where both telecommuting and access to a physical office can be guaranteed, are likely to offer the perfect co-working compromise for both organisations and self-employed. The 2020 COVID-pandemic raised new concerns about sanitisation in workspaces, disincentivising excessive functional promiscuity, hot-desking and high-density; of course, such were the main spatial traits of the office culture 'sold' by the neo-corporate design template [13, 42]. Post-pandemic co-working appears to be prioritising private desks, lower density, dedicated use, longer leases, diversification—de facto amending such elements problematised above. This new approach may reaffirm the more authentic, personalised, local and community-based models typical of the first wave of co-working.

12.5   Conclusion

The global pandemic redesigned daily work habits and turned people's homes into their offices, revealing that agile working is feasible, but not necessarily devoid of problems. The working-from-home experience has shown that many work tasks are better accomplished remotely and independently with clear advantages in terms of work/life balance and productivity. Yet, the case of co-working shows that face-to-face contact and co-location are still vital for fostering creativity, collaboration and a sense of belonging. This awareness will incentivise many organisations and individuals to at least go partially agile, giving workers freedom from traditional work time and space boundaries when task and team permit, together with the opportunity of accessing an office space. Health requirements and physical distancing will inevitably change the layout and the use of both working and living arrangements during a pandemic; however physical boundaries—post-pandemic—are likely to be favoured, as these afford clearer distinction of functions, the loss of which have been problematised above. In this context, co-working seems to offer both the physical and the digital infrastructure to benefit agile workers whilst adhering to their need for community, identity and creativity. What may be imperative in establishing co-working spaces in the future, is in the authentication of the experience, and the genuine alignment with users' values, needs and preferences. Workers who become aware of an insidious commodification of their preferences, or who become conscious that they are being manipulated into playing a 'role' to further a new work script, may become disillusioned and disconnected, potentiating a downturn in demand. It is desirable then, that as we move to a post-pandemic co-working phase, we see a return to the ethos of first wave organic co-working that emerged in the 1990s. Undertaking research into this continually evolving practice is now therefore a necessary and urgent task to help conceptualise and predict novel and appropriate living and working arrangements for the future.

References

1. Costea, B., Crump, N., & Holm, J. (2007). The spectre of Dionysus: Play, work, and managerialism. *Society and Business Review, 2*(2), 153–165. https://doi.org/10.1108/17465680710757376.
2. Dale, K. (2005). Building a social materiality: Spatial and embodied politics in organizational control. *Organization, 12*(5), 649–678. https://doi.org/10.1177/1350508405055940.
3. Dale, K., & Burrell, G. (2010). 'All together, altogether better': The ideal of 'community' in the spatial reorganization of the workplace. In A. van Marrewijk & D. Yanow (Eds.), *Organizational spaces: Rematerializing the workaday world* (pp. 19–40). Cheltenham: Edward Elgar.
4. Edgecliffe-Johnson, A., Morris, S., & Thomas, D. (2020, May 1). The end of the office? Coronavirus may change work forever. *Financial Times*. https://www.ft.com/. Accessed 10 August 2020.
5. Entwistle, J., & Wissinger, E. (2006). Keeping up appearances: Aesthetic labour in the fashion modelling industries of London and New York. *The Sociological Review, 54*(4), 774–794. https://doi.org/10.1111/j.1467-954X.2006.00671.x.
6. Feintzeig, R. (2016, August 15). WeWork to big companies: Work with us. *Wall Street Journal*. https://search.proquest.com/docview/. Accessed 10 August 2020.
7. Fleming, P., & Spicer, A. (2004). 'You can checkout anytime, but you can never leave': Spatial boundaries in a high commitment organization. *Human Relations, 57*(1), 75–94. https://doi.org/10.1177/0018726704042715.
8. Florida, R. L. (2017). *The new urban crisis: Gentrification, housing bubbles, growing inequality, and what we can do about it*. London: Oneworld.
9. Gandini, A. (2015). The rise of co-working spaces: A literature review. *Ephemera: Theory & Politics in Organization, 15*(1), 193–205.
10. Gandini, A., & Cossu, A. (2019). The third wave of co-working: 'Neo-corporate' model versus 'resilient' practice. *European Journal of Cultural*

Studies, 00(0), 1–18. https://doi.org/10.1177/1367549419886060.

11. Gartner. (2020, April 3). *CFO survey reveals 74% intend to shift some employees to remote work permanently.* (n.d.). Gartner. https://www.gartner.com/en/newsroom/press-releases/. Accessed 10 August 2020.

12. Grazian, D. (2019, May 10). Thank God it's Monday: Manhattan co-working spaces in the new economy. *Theory and Society.* https://doi.org/10.1007/s11186-019-09360-6. Accessed 10 August 2020.

13. Halford, S. (2005). Hybrid workspace: Re-spatialisations of work, organisation and management. *New Technology, Work and Employment, 20*(1), 19–33. https://doi.org/10.1111/j.1468-005X.2005.00141.x.

14. Hilbrecht, M. (2007). Changing perspectives on the work–leisure relationship. *Annals of Leisure Research, 10*(3–4), 368–390. https://doi.org/10.1080/11745398.2007.9686772.

15. Jones, T. (2020, April 20). Italian lessons: What we've learned from two months of home schooling. *The Guardian.* https://www.theguardian.com/education/. Accessed 10 August 2020.

16. Kelliher, C., Anderson, D., Kossek, E., Lewis, S., & Hammer, L. (2010). Doing more with less? Flexible working practices and the intensification of work. *Human Relations, 63*(1), 83–106. https://doi.org/10.1177/0018726709349199.

17. Kunda, G. (1992). *Engineering culture: Control and commitment in a high-tech corporation.* Philadelphia, PA: Temple University Press.

18. Lewis, S. (2003). The integration of paid work and the rest of life: Is post-industrial work the new leisure? *Leisure Studies, 22*(4), 343–345. https://doi.org/10.1080/0261436031000159431.

19. Lorne, C. (2020). The limits to openness: Co-working, design and social innovation in the neoliberal city. *Environment and Planning A: Economy and Space, 52*(4), 747–765. https://doi.org/10.1177/0308518X19876941.

20. Mariotti, I., Pacchi, C., & Di Vita, S. (2017). Co-working spaces in Milan: Location patterns and urban effects. *Journal of Urban Technology, 24*(3), 47–66. https://doi.org/10.1080/10630732.2017.1311556.

21. McKee, A. (2017). Happiness traps: How we sabotage ourselves at work. *Harvard Business Review, 95*(5), 66–73. https://hbr.org/2017/09/happiness-traps.

22. Merkel, J. (2015). Co-working in the city. *Ephemera: Theory & Politics in Organization, 15*(1), 121–139.

23. Merkel, J. (2018). 'Freelance isn't free:' Co-working as a critical urban practice to cope with informality in creative labour markets. *Urban Studies, 56*(3), 526–547. https://doi.org/10.1177/0042098018782374.

24. Molotch, H., & Boden, D. (1993). The compulsion of proximity. In D. Boden & R. Friedland (Eds.), *Now/here: Time, space and social theory.* Berkeley and Los Angeles: University of California Press.

25. Nilles, J. M., Carlson, F., Jr., Gray, P., & Hanneman, G. (1976). *The telecommunications-transportation tradeoff, options for tomorrow.* New York: Wiley.
26. Newport, C. (2020, May 26). Why remote work is so hard—And how it can be fixed. *The New Yorker.* https://newyorker.com/culture/. Accessed 10 August 2020.
27. Office for National Statistics. (2020, June 28). *Technology intensity and homeworking in the UK.* https://www.ons.gov.uk. Accessed 10 August 2020.
28. Oldenburg, R. (1989). *The great good place: Cafes, coffee shops, community centers, beauty parlors, general stores, bars, hangouts, and how they get you through the day.* New York: Paragon House.
29. Parker, R., & Bradley, L. (2000). Organisational culture in the public sector: Evidence from six organisations. *International Journal of Public Sector Management, 13*(2), 125–141. https://doi.org/10.1108/095135500103 38773.
30. Peck, J. (2012). Austerity urbanism: American cities under extreme economy. *City, 16*(6), 626–655. https://doi.org/10.1080/13604813. 2012.734071.
31. Perlow, L. A. (1998). Boundary control: The social ordering of work and family time in a high-tech corporation. *Administrative Science Quarterly, 43*(2), 328–357. https://doi.org/10.2307/2393855.
32. de Peuter, G., Cohen, N. S., & Saraco, F. (2017). The ambivalence of co-working: On the politics of an emerging work practice. *European Journal of Cultural Studies, 20*(6), 687–706. https://doi.org/10.1177/136754941 7732997.
33. Reichenberger, I. (2018). Digital nomads—A quest for holistic freedom in work and leisure. *Annals of Leisure Research, 21*(3), 364–380. https://doi. org/10.1080/11745398.2017.1358098.
34. Rodrigues, R. A., & Guest, D. (2010). Have careers become boundary-less? *Human Relations, 63*(8), 1157–1175. https://doi.org/10.1177/001 8726709354344.
35. Rubery, J., Keizer, A., & Grimshaw, D. (2016). Flexibility bites back: The multiple and hidden costs of flexible employment policies. *Human Resource Management Journal, 26*(3), 235–251. https://doi.org/10.1111/ 1748-8583.12092.
36. Schram, S. (2015). *The return of ordinary capitalism: Neoliberalism, precarity, occupy.* New York: Oxford University Press.
37. Spinuzzi, C. (2012). Working alone together: Co-working as emergent collaborative activity. *Journal of Business and Technical Communication, 26*(4), 399–441. https://doi.org/10.1177/1050651912444070.

38. Sturges, J., & Guest, D. (2004). Working to live or living to work? Work/life balance early in the career. *Human Resource Management Journal, 14*(4), 5–20. https://doi.org/10.1111/j.1748-8583.2004.tb.00130.x.
39. Standing, G. (2011). *The precariat: The new dangerous class*. London: Bloomsbury Academic.
40. Thompson, D. (2020, March 13). The Coronavirus is creating a huge, stressful experiment in working from home. *The Atlantic*. https://www.the atlantic.com/ideas/.
41. Tonkiss, F. (2013). Austerity urbanism and the makeshift city. *City, 17*(3), 312–324. https://doi.org/10.1080/13604813.2013.795332.
42. Van Meel, J. (2011). The origins of new ways of working. *Facilities, 29*(9/10), 357–367.
43. Witz, A., Warhurst, C., & Nickson, D. (2003). The labour of aesthetics and the aesthetics of organization. *Organization, 10*(1), 33–54. https://doi.org/10.1177/1350508403010001375.

Conclusions

CHAPTER 13

Concluding Thoughts and Implications

Christine Grant and Emma Russell

Abstract In this conclusion, we acknowledge that a wide range of research and expertise has been accessed to make a significant contribution to academic literature and practice relating to the human side of agile working. We outline key contributions of this book and provide seven principles of agile working to aid organisations and workers seeking to implement effective agile work practices as we move towards a new post-pandemic era of work. We conclude that productivity and well-being, at organisational and individual levels, must be considered equally, to determine what is effective. Future pathways for research are discussed to further move this field of research forward, including a need to explore the innovative aspects of agile working, engage in longitudinal studies and

C. Grant
School of Psychological, Social and Behavioural Sciences,
Coventry University, Coventry, UK
e-mail: christine.grant@coventry.ac.uk

E. Russell (✉)
University of Sussex Business School (USBS), University of Sussex,
Brighton, UK
e-mail: emma.russell@sussex.ac.uk

171

C. Grant and E. Russell (eds.), *Agile Working and Well-Being
in the Digital Age*, https://doi.org/10.1007/978-3-030-60283-3_13

develop alternative theoretical approaches for framing our understanding of agile work.

Keywords Agile working definitions · COVID-19 · Pandemic · Future of work · Technology and work · Purpose of work

13.1   A New Horizon for Agile Working

In this book, we provide a new, comprehensive definition of agile working. Within this definition, the key purpose of agile working is conceptualised as meeting organisational and personal values in relation to market, customer and service needs. This novel definition unifies disparate research on agile working, reviewing multiple terms and practices used within 'human' studies to date. To coincide with this, recently the world has observed the largest naturalistic field study into agile working, with enforced national lockdowns instigated as a result of the global COVID-19 pandemic. Many organisations have turned to remote e-working as a solution to allow work to continue that may otherwise have been delayed or halted. By focusing on the purpose of agile working and observing how the world has adopted various agile working practices under a situation of no choice, it is clear that agile working can provide huge benefits to organisations and individuals. However, the less positive aspects need to be ameliorated to accrue these advantages. Organisations are concerned with the need to retain productivity, whilst balancing worker well-being, as workers have grappled with managing unique personal circumstances during this unusual period. It is likely that an agile working ethos will continue to develop more quickly, given the pace of recent events and changes in attitudes towards remote working. This book represents a review of the impact of digital technologies on agile working and well-being, which has been often neglected in the literature.

Technology is developing at a fast pace; at times, the benefits of these new developments can be slow to be realised by organisations. Yet, the recent COVID-19 pandemic has illustrated how quickly virtual technologies can be employed to support remote work when the impetus is there. Whilst the advantages of remote technologies can be great, with New Communication Technologies (NCTs) and Work-Extendable Technologies (WETs) providing immediate access to work anytime, anyplace, anywhere, there is a need to understand the detrimental impact on well-being. Using technology without boundaries in place leads to a blurring between work and non-working time, reducing the ability to effectively detach from work for many. There is a need to manage technology and work communications effectively, otherwise it can contribute to lower well-being, induce work-related stress, increase anxiety and lead to an inability to psychologically recuperate. The availability of technology does not mean that just because we can, we should always be connected. Employers need to provide 'permission' to be switched off during periods of rest to allow for restoration of well-being and detachment from work. Responsibility falls on individuals to effectively manage their technology use and time but managers need to role model good 'digital' behaviours, with organisations providing support by implementing effective policies and guidance for agile working.

Agile working, at its core, should meet the needs of the organisation and the individual but, given the ability to access work remotely, organisations and managers need to be very careful not to exploit individuals through over-work, negating their duty of care. By focusing on well-being, we can see how practices that might encourage high levels of productivity (24-7 constant connectivity, intensification of homework, etc.) can also be detrimental for psychological and physical health. Organisations need to be mindful as to how this can be mitigated in introducing agile working practices. Having the key purpose of the work (not the novelty of introducing the latest HR practices) at the forefront of decisions is imperative. Creating a balance of performance and well-being for workers ensures that both receive equal status in organisational cultures, which can support more effective agile working in practice. Organisations need to consider how to evaluate the effects of agile working by using measures, such as the E-Work Life scale, to increase productivity and satisfaction by providing actionable strategies and advice that individuals can tailor to their needs.

This book uses a number of theoretical frameworks to review agile working. It is interesting to note that many of the authors have explained and framed their work using COR and boundary theories, in particular. There is little doubt that those who have more resources for controlling and managing personal preferences about how to agile work can improve and build resources. For example, when boundaries are blurred, resources are more likely to be spent and depleted in negotiating such lack of clarity, resulting in reduced well-being. Whilst these theories are important in understanding agile working activities, there is scope to investigate alternative ways of understanding this new work phenomenon. For example, new models of leadership may emerge to make sense of how best to manage virtual teams and distributed workers. Further, needs theories (e.g. SDT) and personality theories (e.g. trait activation theory) could provide some insights into how agile work can promote well-being for people by supporting their values systems and personal preferences. The development of digital-related competency frameworks for employees may also be a useful means for understanding which knowledge, skills and attribute mechanisms influence the work practice-well-being relationship.

Our book continually highlights the need to consider personal preferences about how and when to work, the importance of good management and the need to measure and develop agile working skills and strategies to promote effectiveness. We learn how a lack of consideration about how to effectively implement agile working can result in hypervigilance to stress-inducing work cues, sedentary behaviours, isolation and lowered well-being across a range of factors. In each case, we see that 'one-size fits all' recommendations do not work, and the integration of supportive cultures and norms, clear communication of expectations and best practice, and a trusting, empowering leadership approach can help build the resources and control needed to agile work well.

13.2   Key Principles of Agile Working Practice

When developing an agile workforce, this book concludes that working practices, individual leadership styles and organisational culture need to be revisited and developed to support effective agile working. This will enable agile working organisations (and/or those organisations looking to implement agile working) to take account of WETs and NCTs, fully considering the impact on the well-being of agile workers.

We propose seven principles for effective agile working for organisations and workers to consider:

1. Organisations need to first establish their key aims and priorities before deciding (in conjunction with workers) which agile working practices can be utilised to best meet these needs. Simply introducing a number of agile working practices without a clear understanding of how these meet business objectives and personal values is likely to be ineffective.
2. When introducing agile working practices, organisations need to communicate with workers to see how individual needs and preferences can be accommodated, whilst ensuring that organisational goals can be met.

3. In developing new ways of working using digital communication technologies, organisations need to ensure that practices relating to these are negotiated and communicated appropriately, to manage expectations.
4. Organizations and policy makers should avoid setting blanket policies, as there is rarely a one-size-fits-all approach to managing well-being and increasing productivity for agile working.
5. Workers and organisations need to consider how emotional well-being can be facilitated in the longer term. Heightened productivity that can emerge from engaging in agile working practices should not be at the expense of overall, long-term well-being.
6. Organisations are encouraged to monitor productivity and well-being over time to evaluate (in a changing environment) what is working (or not) and for whom. Being agile means changing practices to meet new priorities and emerging global trends.
7. Workers and organisations are encouraged to foster a culture of supportiveness and trust, developing norms for agile workers to have autonomy and model good practice to embed it within the culture. Leaders should avoid micro-managing, remembering that everyone needs to psychologically detach from work. Managing transitions between home and work is important for all workers, whatever their personal preferences for blurring boundaries.

13.3   FUTURE RESEARCH DIRECTIONS

The recent catastrophic events of the COVID-19 pandemic have made this a very interesting and fruitful time to research agile working. Beyond the pandemic, it is clear that organisations have the ability to change their working practices rapidly to respond to environmental, social and economic changes in society at a global level. Technology provides a means to change rapidly; however, both the advantages and disadvantages need to be considered fully to achieve all of the benefits. It has been important, within this book, to clarify the definition of agile working and how activities are conceptualised within this, to understand and improve worker well-being.

It is recommended that future pathways for research involve measuring all four activities identified in the authors' new definition of agile working, with effectiveness construed in terms of worker and organisational well-being and performance. There is also a need to examine whether any novel theoretical approaches can be applied or developed, to further enhance understanding, specifically in relation to personal preferences and value systems.

In particular, we suggest that researchers and practitioners in this field could now attend to the following:

- Undertake longitudinal studies that examine the longer-term implications of agile working activities on well-being and work performance.
- Use measures (e.g. E-Work Life and E-Work Well-being) to evaluate the effectiveness of agile working and identify actionable strategies on three levels: individual, supervisory and organisational.
- Study how innovation and creativity can be developed through agile working practices, examining benefits and drawbacks and creating new, pioneering interventions.
- Continue to develop frameworks and models that can account for all aspects of agile working and aid distribution of resources effectively.
- Go beyond COR and boundary theory, to provide a unifying theory of effective agile work.

13.4   AGILE WORKING IN A CHANGING WORLD

Workplaces must become more agile to face and meet the economic, social and environmental challenges of the future. Work is likely to change significantly following the recent pandemic and this may lead to significant changes in the way our future work is constructed. This could include working shorter or fewer days and increasing flexibility around hours of work to meet both organisational and individual preferences. Many futurist organisations are looking to transform and shift the notion that 'work' and 'life' are separate entities, using digital technologies to support high levels of integration via innovative tools, cultures and practices. The merging of boundaries of what is leisure and what is working time may become more blurred as wearable technology develops, allowing us to keep close track of work whilst doing other non-work activities. Further, to support networking and facilitate social support, co-working has emerged as a way of bringing together otherwise isolated workers; this may become more dispersed to local communities and hubs as a less 'corporate' model of working is realised. Such practices may impel workers to review well-being needs, and how new modes of work-life integration fit with personal values. It is likely that the future will see a shift in the way that work and non-working lives are managed, with organisations becoming clearer about how to realise the benefits of agile technology, informed by feedback from workers about how to satisfy their needs and mitigate negative effects.

Agile working can involve working in multiple locations. As such, line managers may be less able to monitor the productivity of individual agile workers. Whilst ICTs already monitor our time spent online (e.g. smartphone airtime) and categorisation of activities (e.g. Google analytics), work now involves a paradox of providing workers with more control and autonomy against a backdrop of increasing surveillance and automation. Although an increase in surveillance methods may provide a means for employers to check if employees are logged-on and completing work-related activities, it does not sit well alongside an approach that needs to develop trust and avoid micro-management. Presenteeism may also increase if working become less visible and workers continue to work whilst unwell; managers and organisations need to consider the costs of this and how to effectively support the well-being of agile workers.

Managing virtual teams is a major issue requiring research attention if agile working continues to increase. Understanding how leaders can best manage virtual teams to support both productivity and well-being, especially as technology provides the ability to transcend both time and space, is now vital. Traditional models of teamwork cannot necessarily be applied to a virtual environment, especially when teams operate across cultures, language barriers and even nations. A sense of shared identity and mutual goal-driven behaviours, and a focus on clear outcomes and developing trust, appear to be principles that can effectively support agile working. Communication and the management of expectations and shifting roles are likely to be especially important in a virtual domain. Adaptive leadership styles need to be adopted, as well as tools, to help develop and manage teams in virtual spaces effectively. When virtual teams are highly motivated, this can lead to greater creativity and productivity.

13.5   OVERALL CONCLUSIONS

In this book, we have drawn on a wide range of research and expertise to make a significant contribution to academic literature and practice. We provide the first cohesive, comprehensive definition of agile working (that encompasses four activities), that unifies the 'human' side of agile working. We emphasise throughout the book that purpose is the central premise of agile working. Organisations and workers must ask themselves what they want to achieve, and how agile working can help them to achieve work objectives before embarking on a scheme to implement new agile work practices. This may mean maintaining more traditional applications and activities, if these are shown to be the most useful for attaining work and organisational goals. We stipulate strongly that to be truly agile, all working practices should be regularly reviewed, in the light of emerging technologies and societal changes, to ensure best-fit solutions are adopted. The 'best' solutions are those that are most effective. In this book, we emphasise that productivity and well-being, at organisational and individual levels, must be considered equally to determine what is effective. With this in mind, we have suggested 7 principles of agile working to consider when implementing agile work into organisations. This provides a useful starting point for organisations and practitioners.

The COVID-19 pandemic in 2020 prompted a magnitude of change we could not have envisaged in the era of agile working. The pandemic has had a devastating impact on many people's lives, loved-ones and work; the speed with which new practices have been implemented has been rapid and reactive. Yet, for many, lockdowns have afforded a new era of working benefits, more time with the family, reduced commuting time, digital upskilling, environmental improvement. Organisations have often significantly altered the ways in which they operate, with high numbers of previously office-based workers working from home. It is unknown at this time if this trend will continue but it has led to many organisations rethinking how they can operate more effectively by using agile working practices and reducing physical office space. As economic stability reduces and job redundancies and precarity increases, the workforce is already changing shape to meet future needs. Introducing agile working practices in the longer term may allow organisations to reduce costs effectively whilst retaining a productive, innovative and effective workforce, able to respond to change. The pandemic in 2020 has shown that organisations can work effectively in an agile way and has resulted in the widespread promotion of multiple new technology and digital communications to enable this. The challenge now is for organisations to retain and develop this increased agility by keeping apace of a changing world of work, whilst ensuring that the well-being of agile workers is not overlooked in an attempt to embrace the new.

INDEX

Printed by Printforce, the Netherlands